Writing Spirit

JOURNALING FOR CREATIVITY AND PERSONAL GROWTH

Wayne South Smith

Cover Artist: Kevin Gosselin
        www.kgosselinart.com

Interior Designer: Jera Publishing
        www.self-pub.net

Author Photographer: Teryl Jackson
        www.terylphoto.com

ISBNs: 979-8-9893036-0-1 (print)
        979-8-9893036-1-8 (ebook)

Published by Wayne South Smith, LLC

For my parents, Wylene and Gene, with love.
Thank you for believing in me.

CONTENTS

A NOTE TO READERS

Thanks for joining me. I am happy you're here!

Within this book, I illustrate ways for you to write about life in your journal. I have chosen to share my life lessons through personal stories on cultivating both a healthy journaler's consciousness and a consistent practice. I focus my journaling on various happenings through observations of my thoughts and emotions. Then I write about the choices I made and the results I received, which oftentimes start the process over again. From this, I learn something new—no matter the magnitude or if it's positive or negative—to guide me in subsequent situations. I choose to be affirmative and grateful in my approach to journaling and life.

The term "writing spirit" defines the intimate relationship I have with journaling, inspiring and nurturing creativity to grow a habit toward building a reliable, supportive practice. I experience this as personal spirit that lifts an energetic activity akin to meditation. This stimulates positive growth and interactions through affirmative thoughts and behaviors, rising from both the everyday and extraordinary circumstances of life. If, for you, the term evokes spirituality or religion, you can choose to perceive "writing spirit" through this lens, and according to your beliefs, you likely will. Every viewpoint is valid. It's all good.

In creating this book, I sought memories that best symbolized the concepts and lessons presented in each chapter. Though textbooks and reference materials are vital to growth, I learn and retain lessons in a more profound way when the lesson is grounded in the human experience. Every good novel, nonfiction book, and magazine feature I've read, every powerful movie I've seen, and every inspirational speech I've witnessed has moved my spirit by illuminating memorable paths to growth through metaphor and storytelling. In this light, I have composed this book.

My intention is that these chapters portray ways for you to discover more about where you are in the moment, as well as where you have been and where you are going. Through sharing my path as a journal writer, growing and evolving creatively, you may glimpse your reflection in the sights, signs, and guidance available. Or, through the text, your mind may spark unique memories of your own. Allow these to help you learn to communicate in your journal, using compassionate enthusiasm to empower both thought and writing.

My memoir is filled with childhood and teenage experiences in the 1960s and '70s, offered to open you to times when your creativity was most likely evident, maybe when your spirit played more freely, even if just in your imagination. Similarly, I also write about my adulthood to show how you still possess this same ability with, perhaps, more choices and freedom. If you experienced creative expression as a child, it is still yours to reclaim and build upon. If you didn't or think you didn't, it is never too late to grow a relationship with your creativity. Journal about it. The sooner you do, the faster you will brighten your way forward.

I have included affirmations to encourage your positive thoughts about journaling. Each chapter opens with an affirmation and then closes with a collection of twelve. Also, writing prompts are featured at the end of each chapter to provide a jump-start for your journaling or inspire a hint toward an ideal topic to write about.

Tools and exercises appear throughout the narrative. These are not featured as assignments, merely offers for when you are ready to recognize them, giving you the chance to explore, discover, and play with writing your words as you wish. Whenever a phrase, paragraph, idea, or question inspires you, remember your blank page. Either make a notation—a personal writing prompt—or go ahead and write. Know there are infinite ways to journal successfully, so if something shared doesn't connect with you, remain aware for an idea that does. Even writing the reasons why a prompt or exercise doesn't work for you can reveal next steps. Any of these routes develop your journaling habit.

In addition to my shared inspiration and growth experiences are some encountered on my business path as I have guided others in cultivating a journaling practice. Names and details have been changed while circumstances were merged and blended to disguise identities and heighten lessons.

In this creative nonfiction book, mentions of my family, friends, and mentors are from my personal experiences and perceptions, as well as my interpretations of stories which they shared with me. Some scenes are amalgamations combining multiple interactions, and in several cases, dialogue has been created based upon my memories. Though I exercise creative license, the spirit remains true.

Though this book's message may be life-enhancing, it is not scientifically based, simply a memoir of personal experiences over many years written to inspire journal writing. It is neither intended nor should it be used as a replacement for psychotherapy or other mental health methods or medications. If the need arises, seek a licensed mental health professional. Along with supporting clients in understanding life's distressing situations while teaching coping skills, some professionals encourage journaling to enhance ongoing treatment. Ask your professional for guidance specifically for you on this matter.

Approach this book in the way that suits you best. If exploring one chapter at a time for a couple of weeks before moving to the next chapter soothes your mind and settles the lesson, that's super! If reviewing with either laptop or a pen and pad nearby so you're ready to write when inspired, that's wonderful too! If reading it cover to cover before writing a single word feels good to you, that's great! Or mix it up as you wish! Simply be open to discovering yourself through the writing of your words as you build your journaling practice.

Now, turn the page to begin traveling your creative path, encouraging your journaling, and enlivening your writing spirit.

Happy journaling! Wayne

1

Writing
Illumination

My desire
is all I need to enliven
my innate creativity
and nurture
my spirited journaling.
And so I write.

A Lamp for the Light

Inhaling deeply as I pulled my fingers from the home keys, I sat back and sighed. "Wow," I whispered, feeling my cheeks rise, pulling the corners of my mouth into a little smile meant just for me.

Even 35 years into my journaling practice, it still amazed me. When I woke an hour ago, my mind raced, spinning with worry. Fears overlapped in attempts to outdo the others until I typed up words about each one and then affirmed their opposite. Soon, only a smattering of anxiousness remained as sentences on other thoughts—some positive, others unemotional—flew in and landed on the page of my computer doc.

Fingers tap-danced as my stream of consciousness about now, yesterday, and the day ahead poured out. I felt compelled to write about an email received from dear friends overseas who I hadn't heard from in months, reconnecting as if no time had passed. This familiarity led me to safely contemplate another connection, a new one with a potential second date, as well as my gut instinct that we might not be a good match. Next, I wrote my appreciation on how I felt welcomed into a new community, how I confidently shared my heart, and how every meeting was more fruitful and fun than before.

As I kept typing, logic lined up alongside emotional evaluation, forming new thoughts fueled by my longtime friends and fresh supportive community. My spirit flashed real in the words in front of me. And unexpectedly, my intuition scored the questionable romantic possibility a resounding "zero" which fell—*Wham!*—right on the page. This sudden impact of truth kindled my smile.

To me, my passionate, written expression incited a liftoff feeling of freedom that is one high point of journaling. This practice of centered self-reflection can be laser-focused, mirroring truth in the moment.

I picked up my empty mug, refilled it in the kitchen, and sipped as I returned. I flipped the switch, and the light from a free-standing floor lamp illuminated my desk. I stretched my fingers, then rested them at their usual spots on my ergonomic keyboard and went back to journaling. I wrote how I have journaled mountains of words under this lamp over the decades since my father gave it to me. And like the personal writing I nurture and benefit from daily, I trust this lamp.

Swallowing a gulp of coffee, I reflected on a time before I began to grow a journaling habit, a time when I recognized the need for more light on this 3' x 6' desk surface. It was 1986, and I worked a clerical job Monday through Friday to pay the rent while struggling to commit to chasing my dream of becoming a Hollywood screenwriter some nights. To my left, I would line up notated index cards, inspirational images ripped from magazines, assorted reference materials, and previously written pages alongside pens and highlighters. To the right sat my prize possession underneath its dust cover: a hulking IBM Selectric typewriter with a dozen ball-shaped font attachments, reserved for typing the screenplay. With the desk against the bedroom wall, the ceiling fixture was worthless for lighting my materials, only casting a shadow of my slumped body. The puny desk lamp didn't project enough light, and in this teeny Midtown Atlanta apartment, relocating the desk was out of the question. With only sporadic progress, I began to blame the poor lighting for the impending demise of my dream. Though I was a good writer, my long held habit of playing the victim made me more proficient at procrastination.

Being Sunday, I picked up the receiver and dialed Mom, sharing my dilemma and asking about popping in for a visit.

"Come on," she said. "I've got a roast on the stove, and you can do your washing."

Then I blurted out, "That sounds good, Momma, but I just want to find a nice lamp that makes it easier for me to write!"

"Well, let's get off the line, or you'll have a huge phone bill. I'm sure your daddy can help, so be careful driving."

I rocked out to the tunes of The B-52s blasting from my car radio's cassette deck as I sped 53 miles down the interstate toward home. I knew Dad, an engineer, would know the best lamp or at least the places to start looking, and Mom would likely load me up with food.

Walking into the kitchen through the garage, I dropped my laundry basket to give Momma a hug and a kiss.

She noticed me eyeing her mixer on the counter flanked by sugar, flour, and Crisco. "I'll make a sour cream pound cake after we eat. It'll be ready in time for you to take home a hunk."

I grinned as I headed to the utility room, calling back, "Where's Dad?"

"He's in the yard," Momma yelled. "Will you go tell him lunch is ready?"

After throwing a load in the washer, I went outside and followed the sound of his robust, often off-key singing to find him tending the garden. After he heard my plea over lunch, Dad took me to the garage, a space I felt was just for storing junk and parking cars. I held my distance and unintentionally touched the soft cotton of my white shirt as he turned on a lamp over the oily clutter of his workbench, illuminating a foreboding array of thingamajigs whose only use seemed to be to stain my clothes.

Looking at me, he pointed to the lamp and asked, "You think this'll be good enough light for you?"

Even brightening his workspace, I hadn't noticed it. Certainly, the floor lamp was big enough, but my negative thoughts cast doubt that felt quite rational to me.

Boring! How is this rickety thing going to help you win a Best Screenplay Oscar? Yuck!

Free standing, the lamp rested about two feet above the workbench. This basic dual-tube florescent fixture was housed inside a metal casing with faux wood grain on the ends. Plastic filters on the bottom spread light evenly over the surface, and the half-inch thick, open-mesh diffuser on top allowed ventilation while shining light upward.

He pointed out a pair of electrical outlets in the cross-stabilization bar. "You can plug your typewriter in here."

My doubt led to worry and fear, and these dark clouds between me and ever-flowing creativity attempted to sabotage Dad's generous offer in my mind.

You know it's covered in grease. It will stain the apartment's carpet, and you'll lose your deposit! Never mind that, it's butt-ugly. Say 'no thanks,' take the cake, and hit the road if you really want to be famous.

After scrutinizing it for grimy residue and finding none, I concluded it was hideous, but the light was okay.

"Sure," I said flatly, as if by not showing gratitude I couldn't be blamed when this obnoxious thing caught on fire. "I guess it will work."

He thought it would solve my issue. So to him, form didn't matter, plus this would help my goals as a writer in some way, a path I believed he understood about as much as I did the use of his tools. From childhood, Dad had told me that I could be whoever and do whatever I wanted without adding either direction or judgment, just trusting and encouraging the good in me. Even though I was a college grad, felt I knew it all, and pretended to be an adult, I had no clue how much I had to learn.

As Dad began to prepare the floor fixture for travel, he kindly refused my help, sending me and my crisp white shirt inside to visit with Mom while he removed his tools, moved the bench, dismantled the lamp, and packed it in my hatchback before putting his workbench together again.

Closing the kitchen door, I heard Dad's boisterous whistling as I was engulfed in the sumptuous aroma of the baking cake. Mom carefully opened the oven for the toothpick test, nodding toward the refrigerator. "Saved you some."

I knew what she meant, and I made a beeline for the beaters, gooey with batter. I licked both clean by the time she pulled the golden brown cake out of the oven. She set it on a cutting board to cool while we folded clothes.

"Do you know what cake you want for your birthday?"

"Lemon Cheese, same as the last ten years!"

She proudly smiled, not so much about my confirmation of her delicious cream cheese pound cake layers covered with a thick lemon glaze, but for the sweet enthusiasm I shared with cake batter smeared on my chin.

As I loaded the laundry basket, lunch leftovers, and a quarter of the warm pound cake in the front seat and floorboard, safely distanced from the parts of the lamp, I hugged and halfheartedly thanked Dad. My fear of what I had gotten myself into overwhelmed my appreciation. Then I moved to Momma, kissing her before hearing her usual, "Now, you call me when you get home."

Nodding involuntarily in concession, I cranked my car, knowing how much she worried about me just like her mother—my Nanny—did too. As a child on family car trips in the '60s and '70s, I enjoyed pleasing Mom by making the call to Nanny, giving the operator my dad's first name as to whom I was calling. When she shared, "I have a collect call for Gene," Nanny would say, "Oh, he isn't home, operator," and I would say that I'd call back, then both Nanny and I would thank her. Hanging up, Nanny would know we had arrived safely. Recently, I felt a little guilty, but Mom, who taught me to always tell the truth, didn't see the call as unethical. Being frugal, she felt we needed that pocket change more than Ma Bell, plus every month, we paid the phone company enough anyway.

This instilled habit rattled me as I drove the county roads toward the expressway. I didn't question my participation in their charade, much less understand how their fear was passed on to me, possibly through generations. Tapping the radio's "on" button, the B-52s' off-the-wall instrumentation and kooky vocals drowned out my worries as my head bobbed and I sang along at the top of my lungs.

My car smelled like a blend of bakery and laundromat when I arrived. In my apartment, I made the call and lied to the operator. With food and clothes put away, I stared at the parts of the lamp and considered the assembly process. I had to move my desk, trashing my well-organized bedroom, then fit the lamp back together per Dad's precise instructions. My doubt spawned worries about my inadequate mechanical skills which barely included the basic use of a screwdriver. Plus, the more I looked at the lamp, the more I hated it. I assured myself I would find something better soon.

Once plugged in and turned on, I stopped to admire how it lit the whole room, even brightening the high ceiling. Maneuvering my desk in place, the wood veneer showed every stain and crack but also an inviting luster I had never noticed. Then I sneered at the dust on the typewriter's custom cover, returning to marvel at the light.

Months later, I randomly journaled by hand at the desk under the bright light instead of in bed. And then, as an even-more massive desktop computer replaced the typewriter, I maintained my bitterness that the lamp wasn't my style while still finding additional uses for it. The metal casing acted as a magnetic bulletin board for to-do lists, random writing notes, and silly stuff. The illuminated plastic mesh top became a catch-all shelf for stacks of papers and supplies, even a precarious place to occasionally set a cup of coffee. Knowing a spill could kill the computer's box, monitor, or keyboard, common sense squashed that habit while, unaware to me, the lamp became part of my life.

The computer changed my journaling. Since I loved to record my dreams, I wrote first thing every morning and started to get into the habit. Expanding from slow-going handwriting to fast fingers on a keyboard, I wrote more and more. I even adjusted my alarm to add ample writing time at home before clock-in at my job. Yet unlike my flourishing journaling routine, each time I moved the floor lamp from apartment to apartment, then to my first house and so on over many years, I found it more cumbersome. From my disdain, I became well-rehearsed at pooh-poohing it.

"What a great light!" someone would say.

"Oh yeah, thanks," I would mutter dismissively and then shift focus by pointing out how the front of the lamp was adorned. The display had grown with magnets more decorative and notes more positive. Posted affirmations often served as writing prompts, encouraging my personal growth and the expansion of my journaling habit. These upbeat pronouncements lit positive paths, stating that not only was the journey already underway, its successful outcome was right in front of me. Sometimes, like with the lamp, I missed the lesson.

Over time, my screenwriting aspiration faded as the day job morphed into career, my community flourished, and a loving partnership thrived. The top of the lamp shifted from a parking lot for supplies, covering the light's glow, into a bright arrangement of items of delight, then significance, and then inspiration. Showcased were rocks and shells from day hikes and beach trips; photos and cards that kept my friends and family near when I was alone at my desk; and trinkets from my recently deceased grandparents to support me in grief as I expressed through journaling. Like a family Christmas tree decorated with ornaments gathered through the seasons, this lighted shelf of cherished mementos lifted and loved me.

During the early floor lamp years, I began to embrace my passion for journaling, accepting myself through exploration of both life's highlights, as well as life's shadows. I witnessed the connection between the journaling process and its by-products of better moods and creative interactions with self and others. This emergence felt good, but anytime I veered toward calling the process "spiritual" or "religious," I hit a dead end. A solid wall. Not even a door I could try to open. At that time, the best I could do was write all that came up, including questions like, "Why does this hurt? Why can't I see it? What am I doing wrong?" Then, drained by the silence, I could only type in whispers like a helpless child. "Why? Really, why am I here?" Fully knowing this issue, much less remedying or redefining it, seemed impossible. All I knew was that it was buried and I had to learn to trust my process. I simply had to. So, I reluctantly gave in to the not-knowing and kept journaling.

Over the years, I noticed how my journaling spontaneously enhanced a variety of skills. I realized I wrote words which I rarely spoke. Sentence structure varied as a matter of course. Increased authenticity felt evident as the words flowed, and I began to include dialogue. The writing's speed and ease increased, as did the joy I felt when I sat down to begin. This enthusiasm and confidence transferred to my writing on the job, as well as when, later, I freelanced for magazines, created curriculum for a journal writing class, and garnered a couple of clients in my fledgling coaching business. And beyond always valuing writing for school and career, I came to recognize the inherent legitimacy of personal writing, then began to identify its vast coffers of gifts for discovering self and nurturing growth through my habit. I finally accepted that writing "just for me" was as valid, if not more so, than writing for readers. Even though I never shared the words in my journal, I did share the good vibes this process facilitated as I lived and worked with others.

Like stretching in the morning and regularly swimming laps, I began to view my journaling habit as a practice. Not just habitual, but intentional. Natural and nurturing. Chosen, not coerced. So, I shifted my language on the page and in my mind, affirming my practice. Even when the practice sputtered, just like when a week of swimming didn't include as many laps as the weeks before, I didn't have to "get back in the habit" as I trusted my journaling practice was still there. I simply returned and continued writing. Besides, the term "practice" felt solid in my mind, heart, and spirit, so it didn't diminish. I realized "practice" clearly defined all aspects of my journaling and paved the road for more. My practice had purpose.

In my journal, I continued to write on all that arose from present, past, and future. Soon, I revisited my sparring with some ideas from my religious upbringing, and I slowly began to reframe or release teachings and terminology which didn't feel good. As I ventured onto other paths, I found inspiration, forgiveness, and answers in all services attended, all philosophies studied, and all people befriended. I celebrated living, and I began to feel reassured.

I discovered how spirited I feel when I use creativity, an infinite energy supply, empowering creation. All encompassing, ever-expanding, and always available, creativity continually provided inspirational energy without attachment to how—or even if—I chose to use it. My personality, viewpoint, and passion are creatively expressed by my mental thoughts, my emotional feelings, my physical actions, my spoken language, and yes, my journaled words.

Eventually, I embraced the term "light," a universal symbol of creativity, wisdom, and joy, of highest good, healing, and peace. I viewed light as life, and everything as energy, fully alive energy. Like the fiery core at the center of our Earth. Like the flickering stars at the farthest edge of infinity. Like the twinkle in a baby's eyes. Like you and me.

This light, like the wind, can't be seen, only coming into awareness when it illuminates something else, when it shines on its presence. This includes my journal writing as I see my thoughts outside me, inked on the page.

Now, I see that with Dad's offer and subsequent gift to me over thirty years ago, he referred to the light, not the lamp. Though it may have been unintentional in a similar way that he saw objects defined by their application in our lives, like cars as transportation, Dad invited me to see the lamp as a practical solution for what was most important and desired by me: light.

Sometimes I need an invitation from someone else to light my way. I want a nudge from outside myself to encourage the pursuit of my dreams, to affirm my desire, to move forward and try a little harder, dig a little deeper, explore a little more bravely. If I want it, really believe in it, and begin to pursue it, I attract opportunities and the people who can share these nudges with me. Each is a pebble on the path to the fulfillment of my heart's desire, to discover and shine the light of my life.

Many have encouraged me, and my parents and grand-parents are at the top of the list for all they provided in my formative years. This foundation still supports my evolving goals. They taught me very well through word and example, and I was a good kid who grew into a good adult. Still, for a long time, I thought being taught to say "thank you" was enough. But through the living, sharing, and journaling of gratitude, I have learned it comes in many colors and flavors, that there's depth of feeling and energy—of light—infused in those words when heartfelt. I thought I knew how to give as well as take, but it was a while before I discovered the light in soulful receiving. And surprisingly, despite awareness of selfish behaviors, I was stunned to learn that I wasn't good at giving to myself. I had yet to discover that my act of receiving is where the light pools, and it is from this reservoir that I share with others. Much of my life, I have held a positive exterior—and at times still do—while I was painfully shy, my interior journey fraught with insecurities covered with the Band-Aids of people-pleasing as if loving myself wasn't permitted. I'm still growing, now celebrating how wonderful it makes me feel to share from *my* spirit, not just complimenting or pumping someone else up, but authentically sharing good from my mind and heart to their own.

Funny, but as much as we think we need an invitation to be our true selves, we've had this offer all along. We were born with it, yet some of us fail to realize how significant and constant the offer is to play, to be happy, and to create whatever we want from wherever we are at the time, especially once our childhood ends. Sometimes the offer feels enthusiastic, but the mood is clouded by obligation, anger, melancholy, or fear; still, this goal to create is to facilitate growth and arouse joy. This open invitation doesn't need an RSVP, simply acceptance and action on our part to step into the creative space and start dancing, gardening, singing, teaching, weaving, cosplaying, cooking, painting, speaking, sculpting, loving...or writing. On and on, the opportunities are as boundless as imagination. Determine which feels good in the moment, be grateful, and begin.

Be good, create good, encourage good, share good, love good, receive good...! To me, "good" is an energy that encourages growth in the circle of giving and receiving. The gifts of others, of nature, of intuition, for example, reflect good back to us once we decide to give it a try. Like those on our personal list of trusted ones—a heartfelt friend, caring family member, beloved partner, benevolent teacher, or respected advisor—creativity always responds, inspires, and guides, delivering ideas and opportunities to provide light to brighten our next step. All we have to do is our part: accept with thanks and use the gift. Once the intention to journal is set, we open our senses and gather the gifts of creativity. This synergy becomes our life cycle as we choose to do it again and again.

My journal allows me to externalize my life as much as I like, repeating past and present, even future. I unpack, unravel, and uncover meaning moment to moment, word to word. My goal is to not only enjoy my journaling practice, but to create a better life by building positive ways for kindness and love. My practice frees me to approach any topic from all sides, discovering my best viewpoint toward making a wise decision, aligning my beliefs, and taking actions for good through written affirmation.

An affirmation is a quick assertion of truth—of good already received—a tool most effective when repeated. This reiterated internalization affirming a positive outcome ignites the process of shifting an old belief away from resistance toward allowance of a desired conclusion. Always in first person, affirmations begin with either a powerful "I am..." statement or one with a potent action verb—trust, accept, grow, embrace, create—always in present tense, always in pure, positive language.

A good place to start using affirmations is placing the concept in thought by using it *in* an affirmation, like this:

> I know my affirmation is an intentional statement
> of my desire, firing up my creativity and using
> my awareness to recognize action steps toward
> achieving my goal of journaling.

When I first used affirmations, they felt like lies I told myself. Not a good feeling, truly a fast track to nowhere. Then I began to notice that creativity responds to my thoughts. This intensified as I evidenced how planting these positive thoughts through conscious repetition builds them up in subconscious mind. And when my mind brings them back up within the cascading random thoughts that flow in my head—perhaps giving me an idea or making me aware of an available next step—I feel grateful and affirm this message rising from subconscious to do its good. Next, I stay alert to recognize opportunities and then take necessary action on inspiration, which leads to more steps and eventually—sometimes surprisingly—achieving results. Affirmation not only encourages the process of fulfilling desire through my union with creativity, but this also supports my journaling practice too.

If an affirmation still doesn't seem quite true to you, journal the feelings and reasons why it seems false. This can help you see that it's not magic, that there are steps you'll take to arrive at your goal while using the drawing power of the affirmation. Additionally, your writing will also call up words which speak to your heart and mind, words which will most strongly propel you toward your desire. When you feel the strength of those words, add them into your affirmations. It is also quite legitimate to affirm your achievement of just the first action.

> I feel the desire and affirm I will discover all I
> need to begin journaling.

And then…

> I now have a tool and an idea of how to use it, so
> I build confidence by writing in my journal.

Adapting to make the affirmation feel more real to you grows trust in the process. And look! You have shifted your belief and taken steps to your goal! And that's what it's all about. Now, remember to celebrate it—Yes!—and be heartfelt in gratitude for both the process and outcome—Thanks!—and keep growing.

Along with the affirmation that opens each chapter, a collection of twelve affirmations follow each chapter's narrative to cultivate your journaler's consciousness through magnifying belief and confirming action. In these affirmations, I purposely included phrases from the chapter's narrative to illustrate the transformative power of our words and imagery. After reviewing them, work with those to which you are drawn, or use them all together. Perhaps choose one and engage with it today or over a few days, repeating it until it becomes an encouraging truth in your thoughts. And feel free to adapt any to fit you better. Creatively construct the strongest support to motivate your journaling.

Read them anywhere at any time, always striving to focus on your heartfelt meaning of the words and phrases. Consider reading them out loud. Feel your vocal vibration resonating through your body and all around as you speak emotionally to enliven each word. If it suits your spirit, set one to a simple melody and sing your affirmation. Be playful! Do what feels good as you live these words, feeling them come to life within you and through you. Also, notice them appearing around you.

Ready to write your own affirmation? In each chapter, I encourage you to build this skill and write one. Stay with the chapter's theme, find other words or phrases within the chapter which resonate with your spirit, or go off topic. Even try all three!

Prompts for writing follow the list of affirmations. Each prompt is an invitation to journal, so choose one that sparks you to write. You can even use an affirmation as a prompt. Of course, you can write on any topic you wish. Whatever topic comes up for you—a present occurrence, a memory, or a thought for the future—is ideal to write about. Also, if you want, go ahead and journal from more than one prompt. Get writing!

Notice that as I did with affirmations, many of the concepts in these prompts are from the chapter itself. This was intentional as a way to get your mind in tune to how inspiration to journal is always right in front of you. Anywhere you go in this world, in your mind, in your feelings, or in your spirit holds creative opportunities to discover, examine, and express. There are always rich journaling ideas ready to mine, so grab the brightest incandescence and let the light lead your writing line-by-line.

Some 25 years after reluctantly receiving that utilitarian floor lamp, the switch failed. No light. Panicked, I called Dad. He calmly said to bring it down, so he could take a look at it. I dismantled the lamp and stand, placing them gently in my car, even swaddling the light fixture in towels before strapping it in the back seat with safety belts. Once I arrived, he quickly removed the switch, and we went shopping.

With no luck anywhere, my heart began to break.

Then, he suggested, "I could just bypass the switch and run a plug that you can connect into a power strip. That way, you could still easily turn it on and off."

My spirit perked up, and my worries swooped in.

That'll look awful! It won't be the same!

Yet instantly, I responded, "That'll be great!"

Within minutes of well-trained effort, Dad repaired it, and I packed the lamp back in the car, swaddling and all. He grinned, and I tightly hugged him, thanking him over and over.

After all those years of that utilitarian floor lamp serving a purpose, I remembered my promise to use it until I found "something better." And I finally realized that "something better" was not a fancier lamp but my own recognition of why the lamp was so ideal. This was reflected in my spirit, that even though I didn't fully open to my light within for years, it was still there, empowering me without recognition or appreciation. But once I received Dad's gift in heartfelt gratitude, I made a simple switch and rewired myself, becoming more present to the light and the creativity in my journal, shining from my own spirit. This illumination is bolstered by empowering the safety to explore, the awareness to discover, and the commitment to keep writing in my journal and living my best life.

You are a lamp for the light. You are created of creativity to be creative. You are a luminary, an essential element for expression in this world. Your journaling practice supports your spirit to shine brighter and, through this, expand your consciousness, encourage your growth, and inspire more creativity for you, from you, and all around you.

Welcome to the world of words in your journal as you live in the creative light of your writing spirit.

1

Illumination

AFFIRMING A JOURNALER'S CONSCIOUSNESS

Use affirmations, one or all, adapting as desired.

I am created of creativity to be creative.

I trust the good in me.

I accept the invitation and step into my creative space to journal.

I feel my cheeks lift into a smile meant just for me as I playfully write.

I use the energy I find in words which touch my heart, open my mind, and affirm my new journaling practice.

My journaling always serves a positive purpose. I say, "Yes!" and "Thanks!"

I am human, and like the sun and the stars, I am light.

Knowing growth is what life is all about, I embrace the truth that I am still learning.

I nurture my journaling and cherish its benefits.

As I write my words, I forgive, grow, and create, recognizing self-love.

I am a lamp for the light, an essential element for expression in this world.

I understand my journaling expands my consciousness and inspires creative expression as I bask in my writing spirit.

Write an affirmation about enhancing illumination.

o   Begin with either "I am…" or "I…" followed by an action verb in present tense, such as confirm, magnify, or showcase.

o   Complete with heartfelt words to lift your spirit and motivate your growth.

1

Illumination

PROMPTING A JOURNALER'S PRACTICE

Choose a word or phrase,
and then journal what comes up.

o   Keyboard

o   Hollywood dream

o   Cake

o   A gift which unexpectedly grew in value

Complete a sentence and write more.

o   "I am grateful for…"

o   "I sang at the top of my lungs while…"

o   "When I think of light, I…"

Create your own prompt and journal from it.

o

2

Writing
Practice

My journal is mine,
all mine,
a gift I give myself
to write,
to create, and
to grow.

My Word

E ven through sleepy eyes in the near darkness, I could see him staring at me as I turned on the computer. I had yet to open the blinds and invite in the sunrise, so dawn was represented by the soft amber glow from the bulky screen of my first desktop computer as it sluggishly booted up. Its orange radiance illuminated his hulking silhouette as he desperately darted back and forth, watching my every move. I sat on the edge of my desk chair, scrawling "porthole" and "porpoise" on an index card, before going to the apartment's galley kitchen to make coffee. Returning, I sat down, placing the steaming mug between him and me.

The blinking cursor kept rhythm with his frantic movements as I opened my journal doc and sped to its end in two quick keystrokes. I focused my fuzzy vision on the prompt I left after journaling the day before:

Asleep, Thursday, November 7, 1985,

I gently placed my fingertips on the home keys—left hand on the A, S, D, F and right hand on J, K, L, semi-colon— which was like entering the passcode to open my creative flow.

Connected to this access point, I glanced at my notes, and then closed my eyes, typing the dream from which I just awoke:

> In the tight, dark space below deck on a cabin
> cruiser, I peered through a tiny porthole beneath
> the turquoise waterline, and upon desire,
> I instantly flew through the circular glass,
> shapeshifting into a powerful porpoise. As I raced
> away and jumped high out of the water, I noticed
> the boat I'd left in the distance before twisting
> and plopping back into the sea. Oh, the sprawling
> indulgence as I swam, leapt, and dove…

At this instant, Goliath exercised his mighty tail and splashed water into my coffee.

Angry, I stood up, grabbed the mug, and exited to get a fresh cup, hollering back, "Hold your horses! You'll get fed."

I had rescued him from Emmett, my friend who wasn't tending the muddy tank and happily adopted him out. Still, twenty gallons of clean water wasn't enough for Goliath's seven-inch, cigar-shaped self, and there was never enough food. Yet even with his voracious appetite, he pooped a lot but stayed the same size. I had read somewhere that koi generally remained in proportion to their environment, so to grow, he needed a bigger aquarium.

Assessing that the steaming coffee was still too hot, I finished recording my dreams, then engaged underlining and typed the day's date to mark the beginning of my journal entry. I wrote a description of the splashing incident, how in the shadows Goliath's whiskers looked like Dracula's fangs, then added a recollection of once being compared to a vampire by my early-bird college roommate since I demanded the blinds stay closed and the sunlight stay out until I was ready. I wrote about the atmosphere in my small bedroom, how it wasn't creepy like a coffin, but more like a safe, warm cave. Even though my eyes were hardly open and my body was cramped in a thrift-store bought, 1960s secretary's chair, my nimble fingers pounded out the morning's entry on the keys.

I turned on the floor lamp over the desk, illuminating the small room, and then poured a heap of fish food into the tank. We simultaneously slurped, Goliath his flakes and me my coffee. I rested the cup on the desk and journaled my admiration of his gray battleship shape, how he could suspend himself in one position with his translucent pectoral and pelvic fins that moved delicately like little angel wings. He was my companion, watching over my writing habit these few months, reminding me through his antics that there's so much to take in and so much to write, no matter the size of my space.

Each morning with intention, my journaling began with recording my dreams, then I felt compelled to write more, mostly whining about the previous day or other past incidents. I found free reign in writing "old stuff," and I remained supported, even a little thankful, by doing something good for myself through the act of writing in a journal. Truthfully, whatever the topic, I felt good about this personal use of time, so I wanted to keep writing. Early on, however, as I continued for more days than I honestly thought I would, I began to feel badly about myself when a familiar voice scolded me from the chasm of my mind.

Journaling? How selfish! Momma taught you better!

In my journal, I pondered what expression isn't self-indulgent? And besides, even though she insisted on my doing homework and chores, Momma always encouraged me to play, draw, make up games, and write.

I believe I *am* my life's work. Of course, my journal is self-indulgent! It is all *about* me, fully *from* me, and just *for* me. These words are private about both my outer and inner life. For encouragement, I wrote:

> In my own words and in my own way, I write
> my thoughts, feelings, and observations in my
> journal.

To increase my awareness, I printed several of these affirmations, then placed them on the lamp's frame, the bathroom mirror, and the car dashboard, even tucked one in my wallet for good measure as I would spy the slip of paper whenever I reached for a buck.

My process began to come together. Even when overwhelmingly busy, delightfully vacationing, physically sick, or just plain ole ill-tempered, I journaled every day. Like bathing, eating, and sleeping, this daily action soothed body and mind, a positive way to clear my head while recognizing and centering self for sustenance. Even when I mostly wrote complaints, journaling was still a great way to start my day.

As I shared with others, I quickly learned not to talk about my new habit with just anyone. I found that the most common setback I faced was ridicule when someone compared me, a man in my late twenties, to a nine-year-old girl and her "dear diary." Even many adult women felt that journaling was strictly for childhood. At the time, overwhelmed with embarrassment, all I could say was that my journal is not a little girl's diary as I am not a little girl. Later, I realized the little girl is most likely writing from some desire that she can't quite name yet. Honestly, it was the same with me. Perhaps her diary allowed her to discover this purpose, but even if not, it opened her up to private reflection and growth. Many people began their personal writing journey in their youth, and no matter what the person calls the process or if the person starts at nine years old or ninety, the essence of the practice is the same.

The distaste some have against writing in a diary is that it seems to only be reporting.

"How mundane," they would scoff. "What's the point if the writing just chronicles random facts without examination?"

I wondered if these naysayers still felt the sting of having had their diary read, even having their words used against them. Or they may have felt guilty for doing the same to another, perhaps out of spite or jealousy. The child-writer may only be looking at the present moment or the recent past from an active realm of consciousness, and what a gift. That's freedom, something an adult often has more difficulty finding. But after years of having and hiding adversities, as well as trying new solutions and adapting relationships with self and others, we each have more pieces to the puzzle of our consciousness, of who we are. Reporting is still good and quite valid. Now, we can try to push ourselves further on the topic and feel more expansive.

My friend Roberta recalled her pre-teen years, sharing, "I wrote things like 'Troy isn't cute anymore, but Carlos is fab, and Kabir didn't talk to me at lunch, and I thought I would die.'"

At 38, she found liberation in a writing prompt, encouraging her return to journaling. Soon, she permitted herself to follow the words wherever they wanted to go. As an adult, her content was as rich and varied as her life had become.

My friend utilized both her adult experience and maturity, alongside her child's naïve curiosity. She trusted herself while feeling safe to consider deeper feelings and inquire with complex questions in her journal's wide-open reflection.

Years after moving Goliath to a friend's pond, an antique bathtub sunk into the earth of an urban garden, my swirly-striped tabby cat Claude took his place. After the kitten phase of batting at pens, paper clips, and my moving fingers, he settled in as an ideal writing buddy, often sleeping curled up next to the keyboard through much of my journaling.

By then, I was in the flow of waking with my journal in a less complaining and more compassionate way. My daily practice had solidified, still recounting my dreams and then continuing to write about the previous day along with whatever else came up. Hoping to understand more about myself, I also added free-flowing personal examination, consciously moving toward balance in reporting and inquiry, recognizing prompts arising from my questioning of all angles. This enhanced my writing as I experimented with new thoughts to try and change my pattern of carrying yesterday's reactions and emotions again, even visualizing the coming day as better than the one before. Expansion appeared as a matter of course, encouraging broader thinking while accelerating output and revealing subjects.

Like Goliath grew in double the water and Claude went from kitten to cat, I matured with my journaling. With increased safety, my daily practice not only brought release and fulfillment, it also expanded my clarity and awareness. I better understood myself and the world in which I interacted. This gave me additional good to give others, even if I was just offering an improved attitude.

To get in the habit of journaling, these are techniques which work for me. Hardly rules, these four recommendations came from exploration and experimentation to build momentum and ease of flow in a journaling practice.

Begin Writing

When you are thinking about writing, you may be preparing yourself to do so, but still, if you're just thinking, you aren't writing. Get a blank page in front of you and go for it! Write those thoughts you've pondered about writing. Really, write about anything that's present now.

I believe the best topics are what's right in front of your face, what is in the forefront of your mind, and what circles your heart. Journaling is about expressing your truth to the greatest degree you can, then leaping for more height and diving for more depth. Through truth, insight emerges, often when you aren't even trying to write it. But don't look for it and don't stop to analyze it. Go! If it leads you down a new path of words, pick up the pace and journal all about it.

Write to discover your special way to free up the flow of words without judgment. Just show up at the clean page and face your fear that the words you write might not fill this page, much less the next and the next... Simply begin writing. Amass an abundance of thoughts and ideas, so you start to see the solidity of what you've written, feel your progress, and stand poised toward more.

Oh, no! What if there's nothing to write about? Take a deep breath and journal the first thought that comes to mind. Or write the reasons why you are writing in the first place. What did you have to do to arrive at this moment to journal? Counter fear with thankfulness for your journaling habit and other parts of your life. Consider your new journal book or the fact that you've opened a new document on your computer for writing. Think about how you bought a new pair of shoes and feel appreciation, even excitement, without having worn them anywhere yet. So, where will you wear them first? Be in the freshness of possibility and write gratitude about anything and everything. If you think that's silly because you're stymied, imagine how you want to feel when you are writing vigorously to keep up. Always go where it leads you.

So, now what? This thought accentuates the minute you realize you've run out of words, so be creative with your process. Notice that my suggestions above of taking a breath and writing what comes to mind, as well as the avenues to write on gratitude, are prompts. Simply put, a writing prompt is a topic in the form of a word, phrase, statement, quote, or question that sparks inspiration for journaling. It can also be a photo, a social media post, an event, a sighting, a piece of art, even a new pair of shoes. Anything can serve as a jumping off point to get you unstuck and writing again.

Prompts are shared at the end of each chapter. You can also find these in books or on the internet. Search "writing prompts," adding any further definition you wish, such as "journal writing prompts" or "writing prompts about cats," and watch as scores of them line up. Just don't let the search take over your writing time. Be sure to keep the goal of finding one then beginning to write in seconds. Remember you can write about anything in whatever way you wish, so grab a prompt and go!

You can also capture your own prompts. Keep a pad in your pocket, purse, or backpack, on the desk at your job, on your nightstand, or on the passenger seat of your car to make a quick note at a traffic light. You will develop your own system of writing a word or short phrase in your own code, possibly something no one around you will understand if they see it, but a personal prompt which will clearly take you to a subject on which you want to write. By the way, this is the same method I use to capture fleeting dreams in the dark of night or in the dawning of day, such as jotting down "porthole" and "porpoise." And remember, "Now, I write about..." is a prompt too.

Well, what if there's too much to write about? To resolve the stressful competition for my attention, I place fingertips on the home keys and write a topic list in whatever way it falls out. This list is a roadmap of sorts which helps me relax and trust that every topic has been acknowledged. And then I focus on one which beckons me to prompt my journaling.

And what about other fears? Like any thought, a fearful one belongs to you, and it's fair game to write about. As you do, write about how you are feeling this moment and how you felt at other times around this concern. Be open to the opposite feelings, too, particularly thoughts that are affirmative. If a topic becomes too much, switch lanes and write about something else, perhaps a more cheerful thought. The unfinished thought will resurface at some point, giving you another chance to write on it. And though writing itself can do wonders, don't push yourself if you are in emotional pain. Contact a trusted one if you need reassurance or reflection from someone close.

So, how long do you write? To get started, it's wise to establish either a span of time to write or a number of pages to fill. I began with five minutes and added another minute each session until I reached a total of twenty. In about half a year, I became accustomed to sitting still, being present, opening my mind, and letting my heart speak on the page. I then tried writing a specific length, beginning with one page. Eventually, I began to trust that I would honor my commitment daily without these structures. Later, I trusted that I might type only a small bit one morning, then many times my usual on the next. Over the years, I have noticed the documents of my monthly journals are similar in length.

And when is the right time to write? Well, anytime you are journaling is the best time. Set your intention towards regularity and stability to build a practice that feels natural, that's a good fit. I write every morning, and it feels great. Occasionally, I'll add something later in the day too.

Where's the ideal place to write? Do you need a designated space to write in, or can a temporary spot inspire journaling just as well? I know many who love writing while sitting in their favorite chair, on a park bench, or on a rock off the trail when taking a hike. Others find their words within the commotion of coffee shops. Some write anywhere.

For years, Claude was part of my morning ritual, cozied up on the desk. Messing with things as kittens do, he would often tease my compulsion to keep my desk neat, where supplies and papers were meticulously organized. Clutter makes me nervous, plus I thought I needed a clear path for ideas to flow. Claude brought playfulness to the desk and helped me release some of this preoccupation to focus on what was most important: putting words on the page. Nowadays, I feel comfortable at my desk or making one somewhere I'm visiting. To me, my creativity spills truth onto the page from inside of me, no matter where I write.

To type up or write down? Is it better to journal with pen on paper or to type into a computer doc? Some say that handwriting is more tactile and thus more real. For me, a touch typist since age 16, my fingers on the home keys certainly feel tactile as my mind is centered, plus I write a lot faster. Many feel handwriting is more organic as energy flows down the arm, through the pen, and onto the page. To me, typing does the same thing except it flows down both arms. All my fingers, even both thumbs, are completely involved. They say the pace of writing by hand stimulates the brain to contemplate and dictate more easily. I say that my brain speaks too quickly, and I get anxious while trying to write fast enough, becoming frustrated with a cramped hand and illegible writing. I type about sixty words per minute, so typing satisfies me as long as I stay focused on the flow, not noticing and correcting mistakes or paying attention to the markings my word processor points out. Some say that writing by hand is the way the greatest writers did this, and the "typing up" refers to "typesetting those classics into print." For me, writing is writing, however it's put on paper, and the thought that "typing up" is formalizing and preparing it for others is not applicable to the process of journaling. Typing works for me and makes me a happy journaler!

Surveying journal writers on this topic for well over two decades, everyone has their favorite choice while some utilize several. Truly, I know that I can't be like some who write with their thumbs on a smartphone. Neither the reduced keyboard of a small laptop nor the miniature keypad of a tablet, even the optional external one, meets my needs. Also, some who sit at a computer five days each week find a special privilege in using pen and paper. I have discovered that my desktop with a wireless, ergonomic keyboard provides my best method. And when I am away, I'll use my laptop, if I have it with me, or I'll use a pen and a lined pad, taking breaks to stretch my writing hand. Now, it's your turn to discover whatever feels good to you. And journal all along the way!

In journaling, use prompts and methods that suit you. Write with language that feels comfortable, allowing you to easily open your mind. Choose words which convey meaning from your heart. Remember, you are writing only for yourself, so release concerns of being graded, and for goodness' sake, punctuate as you wish without worries of red ink ever staining your page. Remain present and aware, and then do what works best for you in the moment—and change it up as needed—to build your habit. Trust you will be able to read and relate to your writing when the time comes.

Don't Review

Okay, I feel you! I know this is counterintuitive and very difficult. I was trained in high school and college to review my writing not only when I finished, but many times along the way. Avoiding the urge to read my words as I journaled wasn't a piece of cake, for sure, but I made this a valued part of my practice. Trust me, it's a huge gift to your journal writing process and to you as a writer. Please give it a try.

Especially in the beginning, reviewing your writing can lead to judgment and critique. The goal of journaling is for all-out expression by accessing and utilizing your creativity, emotions, and intelligence without stopping to analyze it. Really, even giving that analytical side of your brain a rest has to feel good! Build your confidence in the flow of process for at least six weeks, if not two or three months, before reading.

Watch using the excuse of losing your train of thought to re-read while journaling. You could read the last sentence, but this most often leads to looking at the one before and the one before that. Better yet just breathe, even rest your eyes for a spell, and then center as you prepare to catch the next train of thought and the words it inspires you to write. Hop aboard!

And if you really feel lost with nowhere to go, remember the trick of being present to begin again. I remember doing this with my cat Claude, describing him as he napped to get the words flowing again instead of taking my fingers off the home keys to rouse and engage him in play.

Try not to evaluate whether something is significant enough to spend your words on. As you write, enjoy the adventure and discovery. Be playful and focus on the process of writing, not the topic or the ending point. Remember on any trek, side roads appear, presenting a choice, and foot paths cut into the woods, hinting of fairy tales. If intrigued, go for it!

Avoid pressuring yourself into inquiry at this juncture. Of course, you'll likely question and analyze without aiming to do so, and that's fine. Just stay in the flow of writing while ignoring the pull to review what you've written. Pausing to mull things over stops the words pouring onto the page. Continuous writing is your current goal, and soon enough, you will naturally fold inquiry into this process. At this time, if you want, simply affirm your openness to easily incorporate inquiry into the steady flow of your writing. Perhaps write that affirmation for yourself.

Even though as you form a habit you won't read what you have written, know that you will one day. There's more in Chapter 11, Writing Reflection. For now, celebrate taking the time, discovering the words, and committing them to paper. Just journal.

Don't Edit

Editing comes from inspection and evaluation of overall expression and fine detail. This critical thinking stifles the creative flow of words into your journal.

If after writing something, you have another thought that seems "better," write that one down too. Don't erase, back-space, or mark through the original words. Either use a slash to show the shift and write the sentence all over again or improvise a quick way to satisfy yourself while continuing to write. Get used to always moving forward.

Never check your written words for proper punctuation. When writing, give yourself permission to punctuate as you wish, even *if* you wish. Perhaps even journal to feel the relief of sharing your personal feelings with the prompt, "Who cares about punctuation?" Your journal certainly doesn't. Or if you feel stymied by some English teacher's dogmatic demands from days gone by, journal to honor this wisdom for other writing while releasing these restraints from your journaling. Merrily, merrily, follow the stream of consciousness without worry of any or all punctuation. This might be a game changer for you, so feel free! Let your words flow.

From personal experience, I have noticed many writers are not their own best editors. Though that's a skill you might learn later, or you might hire someone to edit for you, it's irrelevant since journaling requires no editing. Even if you are a seasoned editor, remember you are not writing a product for an audience;

your journal is for your eyes only. It involves neither editing's comprehensive restructuring and revision nor the concentrated precision of copyediting. Both of these are far too analytical for journaling and—Hooray!—completely unnecessary.

Don't overthink. Have fun! Relax your logic while you develop the creative skill of letting thoughts and ideas flow and flourish on the page. Grow your commitment and make journaling a cherished personal routine.

Keep Writing

Growing a habit is a journey, not a destination. It's being present in every stroke of the pen or tap of the keys with each of your journaled words. Remain clear in your purpose and be careful not to clutter this clarity.

This, too, is true of the ideas I am sharing. They are suggestions, and you make them your tools when they please you. Try them out as you like but keep focused on your desire to journal, doing it in the way that feels best right now. Stay open and ready to try a new approach when you feel the urge. If you can't quite discover it, return to these hints.

If you truly run out of something to write, write about that. Be in the moment and recognize how you feel. Use your senses: what do you hear, smell, taste, and see? What do you feel with the touch of your skin? Write about the size and color of the eyes of the fish staring at you, or the intense orange color of the cat's nose. What song is playing on the radio in your mind, and who's singing it? Be specific; get carried away jotting down details. Or write lists, incomplete sentences, nonsense, or rhymes. Jump from one thought to the next. Capture tidbits of every thought that races to the top looking for attention. Write anything to keep the words flowing. Eventually, you will find a word, phrase, or idea to prompt you to write in a bigger, broader way.

Honor the questions that come up by writing them down. If other thoughts and ideas arise, perhaps even an answer, write those as well. If not, learn to be comfortable writing the question and leaving it unanswered. The answer will show up when the time is right, when you are ready to recognize and receive it. Or maybe the answer is merely living in and writing about the question's mystery.

Honor your frustrations. In your journaling process, if you get frustrated about doing it "right," write these hindrances. Maybe even write what comes up about knowing there truly is no "right" way. And if you're getting nagged by negative thoughts, encouraging you with reasons not to write, write them down too. Then try and get back to letting one thought bounce—or catapult—to the next. Let the words flow from you without calculated direction, only with full intention to write. Remember you are created of creativity to be creative, and journaling is creative in the light that shines from you onto the page. Even when you are writing your troubles, feel the support and enjoy the adventure of your creative process.

You can create ritual around your journaling if it inspires you without taking away much writing time. During various periods, I have lit candles to give me a sense of serenity while signifying a beginning. At others, I've paused to set the mood, attempting to quiet my mind. I've made tea for its vapor, aroma, and the chance to sip before touching the home keys. I have also visualized a funnel coming into my head where creativity poured ideas that flowed from my fast-moving fingers. Still at other times, I pictured inspiration arising from deep within.

I have clanged Tibetan chimes to send a powerful vibrating tone through my body, which sometimes felt like hearing a bell calling me to the table for the nourishment of my words. I've listened to baroque music while writing at my desk, then gravitated toward ambient music, then Native American flute music, and then back to no music at all. All of these encouraged, even entertained, but I always seem to get back to basics where my real ritual is simply beginning, writing in the rhythm of my journaling.

If the neighbors' dogs are barking, the white noise machine in my office is within reach and may be switched on, keeping me centered and calm. Additionally, the earplugs I insert overnight to conquer my light sleeping may be re-deployed. Yes, even earplugs, earbuds, or noise-cancelling headphones can be part of your writing ritual.

Quinn began her practice in my first journaling class in 2003. She committed to a specific time each afternoon, treating her journal like an admired friend as she didn't break appointments and respected their time together by not entertaining interruptions. She turned off her phone, silenced her email alerts, and took her devoted golden retriever out to potty. Once her dog curled up in her nearby bed, Quinn got comfortable in her favorite chair and picked up her pen, ready to have an intimate conversation with herself. She trusts that all is well and the rest will wait. These choices led her to a solid practice of two decades and counting.

Adding gratitude sweetens your practice. To me, this feels as grounded as a treasured ritual and as significant as each breathe. I always finish up with a word of thanks. Sometimes I write this down, but often I just say aloud, "Good journaling!"

Gratitude creates sturdy building blocks for continuity from habit to practice. As you begin to devise your habit, follow the desire to maintain those moments of connection. And if your habit falls to the bottom of your to-do list, it's not a habit anymore. It's a chore. That's when you either "use it or lose it." This doesn't mean that you can't pick it up later. Still, it's like riding a bike, so returning after a break may be wobbly at first.

For now, commit to write regularly. The length of time can fluctuate, but consistently meet the page. You might find that weekday writing times may be brief, while weekend times may be longer. One new journaler with noisy neighbors rose early to finish his morning routine and then headed to the office to journal before his coworkers arrived. Another with roommates stopped at a park on the way home to be alone a few minutes; if the weather was messy, she wrote in the car.

To get in the habit as you build a habit, be creative and give it your best shot to write somewhere sometime every day.

Journaling is about giving yourself permission to exercise your freedom of expression, having the courage to go where it takes you, and being willing to grow through the process. Release stagnation and establish flow, realizing you are not limited like a fish in a bowl.

Just as Goliath's growth was inhibited by his limited environment, we often hinder ourselves, growing only as large as the consciousness we choose to live in while being diminished by the limiting beliefs we hold in our subconscious and unconscious mind. For me, I didn't know I was trapped because that was all I knew. Through safety, awareness, and commitment, journaling granted expansion to recognize and release old, restrictive beliefs and create new, supportive ones. Through affirmation, I grew my habit alongside my life. Ultimately, my journaling went from a short-term habit to a lifetime practice. So, as you develop a practice, consider:

Begin writing, don't review, don't edit, and keep writing.

Years later, I thought of Goliath in his bathtub pond as I toured a rural property that had been for sale and empty for some time. Standing alone on the back porch of the house in the middle of nowhere, I saw a dark pond, the size of the large home's living and dining rooms, and then a lake downhill through the pines.

When I strolled to the pond's edge, I noticed some baby koi frantically moving back and forth, eager for my attention. Even though only a couple of inches long, they exhibited the same "feed me now" excitement I witnessed every morning from Goliath. I felt myself relax as I always do around water, attentive and aware, perching like a delighted cat while watching fish swim. Then I spied an obscure shape emerging in the center of the pond. Instinctively, I held my breath, feeling like this was a nightmare as I glimpsed a giant gray shadow. Without noticeable body movement, the behemoth slowly surfaced, straight up like a submarine, its edges becoming clear, its body a stout three feet long. I sighed, my eyes widening, as I looked at the group of a half-dozen large koi nonchalantly emerge and drift toward me, intermingling with the smaller ones, all ready to jostle for food. I watched this Goliath, amazed at its size, and I contemplated how long it had lived in such a small space.

Pulling myself away, I rambled down a steep path to the manmade lake many times the size of the pond. Looking back uphill, I wondered if a gully-washer could flood the behemoth out, torpedoing it down the hill's Slip 'N Slide to a larger home, a place where it could grow to such a size that I could swim with it, even riding it like a porpoise in a dream. I turned and climbed back up the slick slope, stopping to glance in the pond. All the fish had dropped out of sight. Soon, I vanished too, and the next morning, I journaled the details of this adventure along with the feelings and imaginings it sparked for me.

Just like Goliath fretted and Claude pestered, creativity won't let you forget it's there. It will push, cajole, and tease until you pay attention to it. As you interact in words, it will relax, becoming a beloved ally and playmate. Trust yourself on where to go with your writing. Courageously float along as the channel expands, feel the flow quicken, and then like a fish in vast, voluminous waters, grow through journaling your words.

2

Practice

AFFIRMING A JOURNALER'S CONSCIOUSNESS

Use affirmations, one or all, adapting as desired.

My journal is from me, about me, and for me. Only me.

In my own words and in my own way, I write my thoughts, feelings, and observations in my journal.

I open my journal and begin writing. I don't review my words, and I avoid editing. I keep journaling.

I celebrate taking time, experimenting with suggested techniques, discovering my words, and committing them to paper in my new habit.

I easily access freedom and inspiration when I journal.

I courageously dive beneath the surface, writing my memories and dreams, even the fearful ones.

Journaling supports my growth as I recognize limiting beliefs and create new ones.

I know thinking about writing isn't writing, so I write.

I abide in the truth that journaling nourishes my spirit.

I let one thought flow to the next, not trying to write a story, simply allowing the words to flow onto the page.

I effortlessly grow my journaling practice as I write.

Journaling is a passionate part of my everyday life.

Write an affirmation about cultivating practice.

o   Begin with either "I am..." or "I..." followed by an action verb in present tense, such as interact, cajole, or rescue.

o   Complete with heartfelt words to lift your spirit and motivate your growth.

2

Practice

PROMPTING A JOURNALER'S PRACTICE

Choose a word or phrase,
and then journal what comes up.

- Pet

- Middle of nowhere

- Don't overthink. Have fun!

Complete a sentence and write more.

- "I prefer to (handwrite or type) in my journal because…"

- "My favorite way to start my day is…"

- "I am compassionate with myself when…"

- "Journal writing without reading what I have written makes me feel…"

Create your own prompt and journal from it.

-

3

Writing
Imagination

My journaling
is an
inspired adventure,
growing in
every direction
just like me.

Childlike Wonder
and an Infinite Wish Book

The Penguin suspended Robin the Boy Wonder over a bubbling-hot vat of red-orange goo while, across Gotham City, Catwoman, in cahoots with the Joker, cat-toyed with Batman who languished under a catastrophic spell of toxic perfume, worshipping her. Meanwhile, the Penguin chortled hysterically as Robin held his green-booted feet up just seconds before being deep fried as the announcer said, "Tune in tomorrow, same Bat Time, same Bat channel," and Momma shouted over him, "Look, Wayne, something came in the mail for you!"

Aggravated, I stayed focused on the TV until the credits rolled and I lost all hope for this colorful nightmare to be solved before turning to Momma. Seeing the brown paper package, I knew exactly what it was. Quickly forgetting my favorite superheroes' dilemmas, I jumped up, snatched it away, and plopped my 4-year-old fanny back on the braided rug.

Ripping the wrapping revealed this year's Sears Christmas Wish Book. My mouth fell open as I surveyed the catalog's glossy cover photo of a glowing amber and burgundy Christmas tree with toys piled underneath. The thrill of unlimited possibility rushed through my little body faster than a whoosh of

Santa's reindeer-pulled, package-laden sleigh. I quickly flew past the clothing section to Toyland.

I flipped through the pages, getting a contact high of excitement. I stopped momentarily on the EZ Bake Oven, my mouth watering as I thought of baking a cake like Momma's in my own oven since she wouldn't let me play with hers; the Rock'em Sock'em Robots as I could feel the controls, my nostrils flaring as I fought without getting hurt or hurting my playmate opponent; and the Etch-A-Sketch where my eyes squinted, my brow knitted, and my tongue stuck out between my closed lips as I concentrated on picture perfection. I then marveled at G.I.Joe, his look of determination and vast array of gear from camouflage and paratrooper to the best: the Navy Seal wetsuit, complete with underwater mask and inflatable raft. I could imagine G.I.Joe hidden beneath the waves, swimming with those giant fins on a secret mission.

After begging Daddy at the supper table to write my list for Santa, I was back on the rug in the den playing while he sat cross-legged on the sofa reading today's paper. Tiring from my make-believe games, I spied the triangular opening made by his legs—right ankle over left knee—as a place to slither through to be inside the newspaper tent. I pulled myself into this safe shelter, climbed onto his lap, and mumbled another plea for him to write my letter to Santa. The paper softly crinkled as he brought me in closer, and it rustled more when he raised it again to return to reading. As I closed my eyes to fantasize of toys, Daddy's breathing deepened and slowed. We both drifted to sleep, the newspaper softly descending, covering us like a blanket. I woke up the next morning snuggled in my bed with Leo the Lion and a pride of stuffed animals.

Weeks later, the Christmas tree sparkled in the off-limits living room, and the front door was covered with blue burlap and decorated with a mod display of gold spray-painted driftwood and Styrofoam bells with clappers made of satin balls, a garden club prizewinner for Momma. I paused from playing on the braided rug when Dad sauntered in carrying a yellow pad and a pencil. He sat on the sofa and patted his thigh, inviting me onto his lap. He crossed his legs, propping the Wish Book on his calf, making it my very first desk.

Daddy played head elf, listing all my dream toys on several sheets of paper. I wanted both Tonka trucks and Barbie cars, cowboy clothes and doll outfits, tanks and cradles, games and puzzles, building blocks and demolition sets. I gently brushed my hand across every page like it was Leo the Lion's soft fur before jabbing it with my wee finger, exclaiming, "I want that one!" Then, I paused to ensure Daddy wrote everything down. "And that one too!" Soon, my overzealousness wore me out, and I succumbed to a winter's nap on Daddy's chest.

Within means and reason, my parents aimed to give me everything to enrich my life. They wanted me to know how cherished and smart I was, and though the presents were fun, the greatest gift was their love.

Overall, my childhood was filled with lots of good, but like many of us, harm was done by some of those around me, whether deliberately carried out or unintentionally reenacted through learned habits and beliefs. As a kid, I hungered for knowledge and took in what I was given, often following up with a barrage of "Why?" and "Because why?" I also didn't understand teasing, irony, or nuance which led to some not-so-good beliefs of my own, and these swirled confusion and ridicule before I understood. Others, buried and forgotten, defined me for a long time until I became aware of the behaviors they incited and felt the feelings I had suppressed. Then with the support of my journal and trusted ones, I learned to forgive others and myself, eventually creating and living by new beliefs. Still, this continues, so day to day, I do my best.

As I aged and began relating to my parents as an adult, I took responsibility for providing for myself. This included nurturing my inner child. I believe encouraging this child-like spirit is imperative to a rich, fulfilling creative process. The inner child possesses an amazing ability to explore in boundless ways, always present when discovering something new and always believing in the possibility of "wishes come true." For me, my efforts to be my best and do good for Santa represented this ultimate truth. Now, I witness this from my inner child, and I am the outer adult, the parent whose pad and pencil transformed into a computer journal.

"Inner child" is a loaded word for many, seen as either a clichéd methodology utilized in therapy or an out-and-out woo-woo concept. I see the inner child as each of us during our formative years when we become aware of our sense of self, identify feelings, expand knowledge, and develop personality. Everything is new, and the child is wide-eyed with wonder. Some discoveries might glitter, emitting the pull of a powerful magnet; others might be fuzzy, confusing, or even dangerous. When life brings up questions, the child uses creativity to inspire, imagine, learn, and formulate an answer that feels good and makes sense. And as the child grows, eyes get opened again and again as beliefs are perceived more clearly and adaptations are made.

Being created of creativity to be creative, you were born with a spirit of immeasurable opportunity to venture through a life of language, lessons, and love, which is itself creation in action. Inspiration is your recognition of a special idea from your creativity's Infinite Wish Book. The moment you pick a favorite—That one!—the spark of inspiration ignites, imagination fires up, and your internal playground is radiant, ready for exploration of the idea as you exude your distinctive originality and fuel your light.

As an adult, my inner child is the part of me that remains vulnerable, curious, and spontaneous. Creativity excites him, so cultivating this bond of outer adult and inner child allows the most vivid written expression through the moment's unhindered creative flow, blended with accumulated knowledge, memories, and feelings. When I journal, my inner child and I dream and remember and play together. We believe in the realities of life as much as we trust in make-believe. We harmoniously discover what we want as endless offers for creative expression swirl into consciousness. From this myriad of ideas, inspiration is found, a choice is made, and words are written. From there, the adventure spreads in many directions through multiple dimensions as creative options continue to arise.

No matter your age or early childhood experience, you can access and cultivate this child-adult connection. I accelerated this through personal writing teamed with a special meditation. As a 40-something visiting my parents one weekend, I sat cross-legged on the bonus room floor late at night after they were asleep downstairs. With the house and neighborhood quiet, I perused the box of childhood pictures Mom gathered for me.

I took the images snapped at studios, department stores, and schools, fanning them around me in order by age. In photographs from birth to age five, I saw the light coming through my youthful eyes when the only expectations were to eat well and grow, follow Momma's rules, and have fun. I could see how at birth everything was new to me. With no conditioning or fear, I was enthusiastically committed to cultivate and exercise the creativity from which I was born.

During these early years, I giggled a lot. Also, I was visually impaired, and no one knew it. I certainly didn't know I couldn't see as well as others since I had no reference point to 20/20 vision. I could fly high on my swing set and race around the backyard without running into trees, plus I played games, watched TV, and colored a lot.

But when I entered the first grade and sat toward the back of the class, my teacher noticed I couldn't see what was drawn on the blackboard. I was embarrassed when she moved me to the front row and even more so when I admitted I still couldn't see what was on the board. That afternoon, Mom picked me up and took me to a grouchy eye doctor who puffed on his cigar while examining me. I was timid, and when chided by him, I had to shout my answers about the shapes I saw projected across the room through inky swirls of smoke. I didn't fully understand why I got a pair of glasses with one clear lens and one darkened lens, feeling that somehow a "lazy eye" was my fault for not doing a good job with my vision. The awkward pair of glasses was my punishment.

With better vision, I began to see the true meaning of "handsome" in others while I was called names like "four eyes," "snaggletooth," and "sissy." When school picture day came around, I wore my favorite shirt, and Mom gave me permission to take off my glasses and hold them tightly in my lap when my turn came with the photographer. Now that my "good eye" had been shuttered for months and a bright spotlight was shining in my face, finding the camera wasn't easy, piling on more shame and regret. In these photos, I could see how self-conscious and inhibited I felt in elementary school. It was difficult to look lively for many reasons. Even wearing glasses brought fear which restricted physical play through increased risk of breaking them, upsetting Momma, and costing my parents more money.

In my meditation, I recalled that the child models photographed in the Sears Wish Book were having fun without looking fake, silly, or stupid. Unlike me, I believed they were perfect and didn't get called out for "acting ugly" when their inappropriate actions or misguided humor went beyond unspoken boundaries, like when I was five and we moved to a brand-new house. I was told to "go outside and play" and "stay out of the way," but the only plaything I found was crayons—no paper—so I drew a few little red circles on the concrete step from the carport before Momma caught me as she darted out the door, doing one of her many duties. Immediately, she scolded me and then searched for cleaning supplies, scrubbing the stain with all her might. Horrified at the mistake I'd made, my shame became even worse when she gave up, leaving remnants of my wrongdoing on display for everyone to see just before they entered our home. Guilt overwhelmed me, and I don't recall playing anymore until my toys were unpacked. I was fearful of playing the wrong way.

I unfolded my legs and stretched out on the bonus room's carpeting, careful not to mess up my photo display. Breathing into the process, I heard an opposing thought.

This is dumb. Put away those silly pictures and go to bed.

Rubbing my legs and ignoring my doubt, I noticed in school pictures after the first grade, even one taken my freshman year in college, I forced a phony smile which showed the demands for this photo as pretend perfection for posterity. There was pressure to look my best, yet with the scorn piled up inside, faking it was the best I could do.

Through this meditation, I quietly scanned these photographs of me from birth to young adulthood, simply letting thoughts float through my mind without judgment or attachment. I visualized my child-self sitting on my lap ready to engage, his little head resting on my chest, one ear to my heart. In my mind, I lovingly, yet firmly, told my little boy that I no longer accepted someone else's opinions on handsomeness and ugliness. I affirmed that, as an adult, I would deflect other's misguidedness, jealousy, and cruelty since all that stuff belonged to them, not me. And I would do my very best to grow, aiming to share my good.

In my journal, I wrote what arose from the contemplation. I began a process to heal confusion, disappointment, and hurt while uplifting uniqueness, wisdom, and creativity. Life is a school, and every day is picture day with moments to live fully aware, to discover, celebrate, and build upon. Every moment offers a choice for new creation. Within me, I visualized the perfect environment for my child's heart and spirit to safely play in, and I noticed the truth that my inner child desired freedom to express, experiment, learn, and enjoy. As I fully felt my inner child's presence, I noticed myself letting go of "big words" since simple language did the job to clearly communicate. In my journal, there was no one to impress. The writing itself—the clarity of thoughts and feelings—was the gift meant just for me. I understood and embraced more of the beauty of my childlike state of mind.

In the pictures taken on Santa's lap, my outer adult felt the tradition while also recognizing the utter phoniness of the fake beard and the man underneath it playing a part. Still, my youthful face exhibited a spark of belief in this symbol of the protector of dreams, the encourager of good, and the giver of gifts. I realized as a child I was in awe while also intimidated.

I journaled about how my child-self was secure before falling into the trap of being overwhelmed and questioning belief. He had suffered emotional bullying that echoed in his impressionable mind, arguments thrown like grenades such as, "Santa won't bring you anything 'cause he saw what you did!" This left him desperately grasping to remember what he'd done wrong, even after he asked Momma and she hugged him, saying he'd been good all year and Santa would visit him. And any muttering to stand up for himself was often met with a swift physical challenge, often growled by a bigger kid, like "Tell it to my face, punk!" Anger tightened his little undeveloped muscles and fear filled his eyes with tears which he tried to hide. If this was impossible, he would quickly flee, hearing the taunts of "Run, crybaby!" A feeling of being different from others haunted him, so playing the victim was his only protection as his emotional responses were stronger than his physical ones. He usually found safety with adults more than children, especially those older and larger than him.

And with constant teasing from multiple sources like "There isn't really a Santa Claus, stupid!" my child toiled doggedly to defy logic and maintain belief, even as he recognized each store Momma took him into had a different Santa. Even if the "fake" Santas were elves, he knew in his mind that the real bearded man couldn't circle the globe delivering all those gifts in a single night. Still, he struggled, holding tightly to his feeling that magic exists, and no one could change how real Santa felt deep down in his heart.

Santa symbolized the cosmic goodie machine, the manifestation of "ask, believe, and receive." I often wondered why I could trust this principle as a child but struggle with despair around it as an adult. Though exciting, this power of choice—affirming a desired outcome, releasing it, and then, through action, nurturing a belief to become real—had turned terrifying, even paralyzing, when dealing with doubt, worry, and all the reasons denying the truth. Since I knew imagination ascends from that point where all is new and possible, I agonized over where my playground had gone. The jolt of most every glistening idea was met with a dismissive thought.

What's the use?

My child's spirit was silenced.

So, this place in my mind was as real to me as the North Pole or the Bat Cave, except filled with condescension, censorship, and hopelessness. Monsters under my bed were nothing compared to this intense fear. Although inspiration was ever-present, hostile thoughts evolved, gaining power and voice in my mind, becoming fully entrenched negative beliefs which short-circuited imagination and blocked ideas.

Nope. Won't happen. No way, not ever.

I came to call these internally-voiced thoughts "Never Mind," and this ugliness became my personal persecutor of creativity. My chimney was no longer on Santa's route.

Frightened by this awareness, I realized I had to become Santa to myself. When I doubt my power to create, I poison that purity and oppress the opportunity. Creation is inevitable, and it's through creativity—always accessible, always at the ready—that I can take inspiration and use my imagination to defy the fear and return to trusting the use of my personal creative abilities. Once again, I can fully express my spirit.

I learned to love and protect my child in ways only I could provide, and I encouraged safety in his playground to let him explore and create in any way he wished. Plus, this allowed me to safely ponder the depths of truth, fear, forgiveness, compassion, growth, and empowerment in my journal.

Becoming this Santa-like guardian as an adult authorized me to face my pessimism in a new way. I joined the forces of the child's creative gifts with my current insight to stand up to fearful beliefs that had infected my thinking. Like G.I.Joe and Batman, I acquired special tools to vanquish some negative beliefs and vault over others that seemed impenetrable. Yes, these mental villains fought back. Sometimes this became unruly in my mind, but now I was armored on the front lines with my magical child safely shielded within me.

The opening battles were like those when I felt shame for a physical condition that I was born with. The attacks on my young self were something I couldn't handle, so I stuffed them away where they continued to make me feel less-than and think I was not good enough. Gloomy contempt overrode and diminished my innate creativity. Anxiousness tormented me as I tried to solve it, and as depression darkened, I often gave up.

Sadly, this was submission—a full resignation and total loss—not surrender. Unlike the commonly held belief of surrender as a white flag of defeat, signifying powerlessness, I know there's power in surrender through trusting sparks of inspiration and enacting the potential of imagination. One way I witness this is through my use of affirmations. Writing and releasing the pointedly positive beliefs must include imagination. Then, I follow with surrender to the power of creativity, having confidence to recognize, accept, and take the offered steps to my desire. Surrender is truly an empowered act of letting go to permit good, trusting in its receipt, and then using its gifts to create and grow. Submission, however, is its opposite by completely conceding failure.

Surrendering to the power of creativity also reinforced my attitude to more readily receive guidance and new ideas from all types of resources. Since no one read my journal, this was an inside job with confident movement already underway. Additionally, it positively affected communication in collaborative projects, social connections, and writing in general.

I could gracefully accept these outside offers of inspirational thoughts as an adult without jealousy, defensiveness, and any other disruptive playground behavior. Even for ideas I knew weren't suitable for me at the time, I would accept them with gratitude, not just for the offer, but also for a possible gift of inspiration down the road. From these interactions, I began to kindly share relevant offers with my child through language and feelings he understood, allowing a vibrant expansion of imagination's play in creativity.

In the wonderful land of imagination, there are no real villains, only lessons spurned and unlearned. These will continue to infiltrate and irritate, even terrorize, until you fully face them in your journal, dealing with what their messages say to you as outer adult and inner child. Use your imagination to shift these shouting shadows by believing in something new, something that aligns with and affirms the good in you. Broaden both your security and superhero-like power to create as you grow with your journaling practice.

On the fourth Christmas of my life, I woke up and dashed to the living room in my footie pajamas to find my own unique demonstration of heartfelt desires. I ripped into the colorfully wrapped presents under the tree and began to make merry. Swept up in each second of the big day, neither had I made comparisons to my list for Santa nor had I experienced doubt of not getting what I wanted because I wasn't attached to specifics. Though I grinned while Daddy listed almost every toy available in my letter to Santa, I really just wanted to have fun. I'd forgotten about the G.I.Joe Frogman and EZ Bake Oven, which I didn't get, while I was fully present with each gift I received, including a record player and some 45s, even "The Twist" by my favorite singer, Chubby Checker. All the presents were surprising, ideal outcomes which added to my sole purpose to be jolly.

After the Christmas feast, the black-and-white TV hummed and the fire in the fireplace crackled while Daddy slumped on the sofa, sawing logs. I sat on the rug at his feet coloring the red, green, and yellow costume on the Boy Wonder in the *Batman* coloring book Santa left in my stocking. I noticed Daddy's arms relaxed at his side, his head back, and mouth agape. Even as he slumbered, I felt safe and loved in his presence, so I turned back, picking up a different crayon to color both inside and outside the lines.

And on a Christmas many, many years later, alone in my home with a tree loaded with ornaments, I made a precious discovery. When hearing a song about the light of a child, I breathed into my heart and connected to the spot where it first came to life. This tiny heart—alive with the essence of creation—thumped in my grown-up chest, supplying energy for movement, for emotion, and for thought. I realized, too, these are the same eyes that scoured the Wish Book, now seeing with bifocals, and the same fingers that colored with crayons, now more agile for writing in my journal. Grown yet still growing, it was the first time that my inner child didn't feel beside me or on my lap. Mind, heart, and spirit…we were one.

Inspiration ignited, I left my twinkling Christmas tree to sit at my desk, feeling at home under my lamp's embracing light. I wrote about my discovery and kept writing as more good came forth. Right before my eyes, I witnessed in my words how journaling is imagination in action. I had set myself free years before when my youthful spirit began to return and my imagination was present in all my words, both those typed up to get off my chest and those elaborated upon to capture every angle and emotion. Imagination was present on my ambles down clear paths and around sloppy detours, in the stories rising from memory and those emerging from the land of make-believe. And the union of child and adult in my spirit warranted the full spectrum of my imagination's truth. The journal itself was my coloring book, a bounty that keeps giving every day.

Creativity *is* infinite possibility. Do your best to remember your childlike curiosity and playfulness. Reawaken it or reimagine it with your adult wisdom and whimsy. Like a loving parent, adore your inner child. Integrate, and you will simultaneously embody both starry-eyed child and jolly Santa, forever as one. Open your journal, view your creative opportunities, choose your inspiration—I want that one!—then light up your imagination. And write and write with your writing spirit, watching as the gifts of the present come true through you.

3

Imagination

AFFIRMING A JOURNALER'S CONSCIOUSNESS

Use affirmations, one or all, adapting as desired.

My imagination ascends from innocence where all is new and possible. I play with this precious toy as I journal.

When I write, my inner child and I dream and remember and play make-believe.

Through little and big words alike, I illustrate originality in my journal.

Life is a school, and every day is picture day to live fully aware and then put the experience onto the page.

My writing supports me as I venture through a life of love, lessons, and learning.

I wisely wield my wondrous imagination within my journaling practice.

Creativity is infinite possibility, and I enthusiastically express my creativity in words.

I connect my childlike curiosity and playfulness with my adult wisdom and whimsy as I journal.

I safely write from my deepest place, pondering the depths of truth, fear, forgiveness, compassion, growth, and empowerment.

I color inside and outside the lines with my words, journaling both the familiar and the fantastic.

I am a superhero. I am living creativity imagined from pure inspiration.

I write today and tune in tomorrow to journal again.

Write an affirmation about amplifying imagination.

o   Begin with either "I am…" or "I…" followed by an action verb in present tense, such as marvel, visualize, or glisten.

o   Complete with heartfelt words to lift your spirit and motivate your growth.

3

Imagination

PROMPTING A JOURNALER'S PRACTICE

Choose a word or phrase,
and then journal what comes up.

o   Giggles

o   A favorite childhood TV show

o   My very first desk

o   Wish

Complete a sentence and write more.

o   "As a kid, I exclaimed, 'I want that one!' about…"

o   "I imagine…"

o   "I changed a belief for good when…"

Create your own prompt and journal from it.

o

4

Writing
Safety

I confidently
and
securely
write
the truth
in my journal.

FLOATING IN ICED TEA INLET

Standing knee deep in less than a foot of water, I glanced up at the pine-shaded beach and saw my parents sharing a quick kiss. As Daddy walked toward me, Momma waved and shouted, "Watch where you step!" I looked down at my feet, squished in the muddy sand of this concealed cove off the bay, away from the ocean. The red-brown water was the color of the sweet tea Momma made every day. I felt a shell under my foot and excitedly grabbed it with my toes, causing clouds to billow. Once in hand, it wasn't as pretty as I imagined.

Daddy sloshed up to me, pointing ahead. "C'mon, Sport. This'll be fun, I promise."

I tossed the shell and joined him, watching the small ripples on the surface from my movement and the larger rings coming from Daddy. As I wondered if we were going to wade the million miles across to the other side where skinny pines stood just like the ones we were leaving behind, doubt thundered in my head.

Ya'll will never make it back in time for supper.

My white t-shirt—the sunscreen of the '60s—suctioned to my little chest as it soaked up water. I stopped, squinting to look back at Daddy, the water barely wetting his swimsuit.

"Keep going," Daddy encouraged. "It's alright."

I walked until the wind's wavelets lapped my neck and fear swam circles in my mind.

What if you step on a snapping turtle and it bites off your toe? Or you get swallowed up by a whale?

"Okay, this is real easy," he said as he gently lifted me by my waist.

I knew he wasn't about to pop me in and out of the water, an action that made me snicker. This was something different. He laid me face up on top of the water, and when the water rose around my head, I squirmed, but Daddy didn't dunk me.

"I'm not going to let you sink," he said softly with a reassuring grin.

The water entering my ears felt weird as Daddy moved one hand to the back of my neck and positioned the other at the top of my fanny.

My arms and legs started to flail about.

"That's good," Daddy said. "Your body knows what to do, but let your mind tell it to relax."

I tightened my muscles and didn't move.

"Now," he said calmly, "be still and just float."

I could feel his hands leaving my body, and my heart raced. I shrieked.

"It's okay," he said, taking hold of me again. "I'm right here. If you relax, you'll float."

I tried again, struggling harder not to move. I could feel his palms pull away, then my body began to sink. Through the water in my ears, I heard him say, "Breathe in real deep."

I did as I was told, and he said "good" as I felt my body lift enough to separate from his fingertips. As I exhaled, I began to go under again and panicked.

He put his hands back for support. "It's okay. You will rise up and down, but you won't sink as long as you relax and breathe."

My terror subsided, and on my next try, I got it. Weird, but doing nothing was really doing something. The feeling of being solid, yet buoyant, was surprisingly fun. My body stayed afloat like an ice cube in a tumbler of tea, one that, even when swirled around, always rose to the top.

"Now, close your eyes and keep breathing."

Even as his hands slipped away underneath me, I could still sense his presence. I noticed the sun was hot on my front side and the water cool on my back. With my ears underwater, I could hear each breath inside my head coming in and going out. Floating made my body into a magical boat, resting and playing weightlessly. My mind began to wander to fantastic lands.

I opened my eyes to see Daddy, and he wasn't there. When I inhaled to scream, water flooded my mouth. Instantly, Daddy's strong hands pulled me to his chest where I wrapped my arms around his neck, coughing as he patted me on the back.

"You're okay, you're okay," he repeated. "You just floated away from me a little, but I was watching you the whole time. You were doing everything right, Sport. Really good."

We looked at one another, and when I smiled, he asked, "Ready to try again?"

He helped me onto my back, then immediately slid his hands away but kept talking to me. Listening to him was like he was talking from behind a door.

"We'll practice floating, then I'll teach you how to swim. All you need to know to stay safe in the water is how to float. Your body will always come back up to the surface if you relax and believe it will."

Soon, I learned to push myself from standing to a floating position and knew that I could not only float, but I wasn't in water over my head because my toes touched the mushy bottom. Daddy began to watch me and wave from the beach, best I could tell without my patch-eyed glasses. He trusted me, and I knew I was safe by myself.

Just like a human needs skill to be well in the water, safety is fundamental to developing the consciousness of a journal writer. You find your truth, and in turn, your true voice as you write. To do this, you must learn to be open to everything that you are: all your beliefs, desires, dreams, and fears. You have to become vulnerable within yourself while simultaneously feeling secure and confident enough to write authentically. Whether life is calm or chaotic, you trust you are safe floating on the sea of your words.

For many of us, being vulnerable generally means "easily hurt" or "open to attack and criticism." However, it also means being "sensitive." Vulnerability does not have to be about powerlessness or submission. Vulnerability is surrendering to your desire and the power of creativity to try something new, something you feel will be good once you employ safely to venture forward. Though it doesn't necessarily make the experience easy, safety can certainly smooth the waters.

In relationships with others, as well as the one you have with yourself, vulnerability brings a risk factor often involving situations which provide lessons and nurture growth. So, if risk leads to harm or breakage, consider this as an opening for exploration or room for expansion. The key to releasing fear is realizing that you can be vulnerable while also enhancing the protection of your heart through self-love. This process may increase your sensitivities which, yes, can be reactive like your fears but also can be a delicately beautiful exercise in self-compassion.

When most think about vulnerability, they remember a relationship where they offered their heart and were hurt. Yes, that's one consequence of vulnerability, but we know that being vulnerable can also end happily. Consider a personal expression of vulnerability, opening up and learning to love all of who you are in this moment. If relationships are important to you, start with the one you have with yourself. Strengthening self-acceptance fortifies the foundation to construct future relationships.

As a journal writer, be your own best friend. Trusting you are created of creativity to be creative, fully support yourself while experiencing the challenges and growth that occur through the process of journaling's discovery. The most powerful themes and energy that you put on paper come through self-exploration, through a confluence of the waves of knowledge, feelings, and truths. Journal all sides of your deepest sensitivities. These words are your innermost thoughts, so they need to be kept safe from others. Therefore, write authentically in your journal, knowing the words are for your eyes only.

Throughout decades of journaling, my practice has always been just for me. When I started, I had never experienced anything like this depth of personal honesty before, and I reveled in the process of sharing with myself.

To attain this level of truth in a journaling practice requires an attitude of vulnerability where safety is paramount. Be sure to take the steps to trust yourself in the process. If you write in a bound journal or notebook, consider where it can be safeguarded from the eyes of your partner, roommate, child, parent, guest, housekeeper, and so on. If you write on a computer, consider password protection, or keeping your journaling documents in the cloud's secure storage or on a thumb drive hidden away, perhaps under lock and key.

Safety is not something you ask for; safety is something you claim and protect. For instance, when I lived with a partner, we agreed our relationship was built on trust. I never password protected my files on our home computer, trusting they would not be read. I shared that I felt I would know if my journal had been read by topics and sentiments raised; a violation of trust of that magnitude would be a serious betrayal. Once agreement was reached, we both journaled privately on one computer. And after 17 years, the relationship ended, but this had nothing to do with any breach of confidence concerning our individual journaling habits. In fact, my practice supported me through the tough times leading up to the split and beyond.

In a class where I taught journaling and participants discussed the process without sharing their intimate writings, Zoe admitted keeping her journal in her purse to protect it. Upon hearing this, Stanford said that the purse might be pilfered and the journal read. He added that he keeps his in the trunk of his car, the only place it feels safe to him. Zoe replied that the car could be stolen as easily as a handbag. These scenarios brought up questions about relationships and fears they both pondered in their journals before coming to comfortable terms.

Stanford voiced another common fear. "What if I die and someone reads my journal?"

Playfully, I responded, "Well, you'll be dead, so what will it matter?"

After the group's nervous laughter subsided, I suggested they share their final requests with their trusted ones, such as family members or close friends. They also could leave instructions in the front of their journals or at the top of their journal's computer document with their wish for the words in case of death.

In another conversation, Peg shared that she makes sure her pre-teen children are all right, busy with homework, screens, or friends, then she hides away for a few minutes in a storage area in her half-finished basement to write her thoughts on a small, lined pad. She always leaves the first pages blank to make the pad look unused and keeps it stuffed in a box of holiday decorations. When the house is empty, she journals in various places on one of the other pads she's tucked away, and when interrupted, she shoves it upside-down into a nearby drawer, under the sofa, or in the spice cabinet in the kitchen. I asked if she was concerned her words would be read.

"I haven't thought about that in years. The journals are hidden well enough. I also know where my kids dig for things they want, plus a pad is never one of them."

"So, would you encourage your partner to find and destroy them if you passed on?"

She thought briefly, then answered confidently, "No. If I die and she finds them, it's her choice. I'm okay with that."

I nodded and noticed as she shifted her gaze to catch another thought.

"Huh, I have never thought about this before," she said, looking back at me, "but you know, maybe even some things unsaid in life could be communicated through my writing after death."

"Interesting. So, do you ever think about that when you're journaling?"

"Oh, goodness no," she replied, brushing off the question with a wave of her hand.

I sat back and considered that this could be a huge gift to the grieving and, who knows, perhaps a huge relief to her once she's passed on. And as long as she's clear that it's not an intention while she's alive, her practice remains healthy. Her only goal is securing her safety for privacy to write now.

I have a provision in my will as to who will inherit my journals, as well as every other word I've written. My executor and I have discussed the details of what's to occur at that time. To me, just as I have made decisions for my physical body, I have the same for my body of personal writing. I want to responsibly leave a path for next steps, and I feel confident that the one I have left will take good care of it. For me, that's a peaceful feeling.

All of this is a personal decision. I felt safe in my journal writing, and I wrote for decades with a "let it be" attitude before deciding to add instructions to my will. You'll know when and what you need to do. Get to a place of trust. Don't let this stop you or interfere in your thoughts and actions to journal. Claim your safety and move ahead with honesty in your practice.

Though I don't recommend sharing your journal, I knew the camaraderie from teaching classes and participating with others as we shared space while journaling with no expectation of discussing the contents. For Aubrey, this was especially profound. As a single mother who built a heartfelt practice over a few years, she wanted to encourage her son to trust his writing and grow awareness abilities. So, they sat in the living room—her with a laptop, him with his tablet—and journaled. Once finished, they never talked about what came up in their writing. They also didn't speak much about how this act made them feel. She witnessed him being introspective and relaxed which lessened her anxiety about him as a teen, and he enjoyed quiet time with his mom. Still, it bonded them in relationship through sharing this soulful activity. They often moved on to cooking or running errands together, and Aubrey noticed that their chats were a little more carefree.

Again, here's the bottom line: you must feel safe to write and secure that no one else is going to read your journal. No one's going to grade it or judge it or challenge its words. It's not for mass consumption, and it's not for sale. Your journal is just for you. Period.

Like when I was learning to float, whenever we try some thing new, we are often hypersensitive to every way this could go wrong before discovering how it could go right. Some of these reactions are healthy responses. However, be aware that Never Mind wants to drown out the more positive thoughts by frightening, shaming, or guilting you. Seems strange but providing personal safety from outside risks is sometimes easier than providing safety from what comes up in our own consciousness.

To write your truth, learn to not shut off your expressions due to personal judgment. Boldly write whatever comes up for you, including the condescending mental messages of Never Mind. Don't concern yourself with where these originated or what they mean. You may receive answers or formulate conclusions later. For now, write them alongside other thoughts while strengthening your habit and its expression by continuing to journal.

Learn to listen to yourself with compassion, allowing the exploration of some situation or feeling without judgment, if you can. Write as it comes, then move on. And like my father's kind yet firm encouragement in teaching me a new skill, cultivate a soft, loving internal voice when you speak to yourself as you journal. Know there is creativity in every word. Listen to your gentle urgings to write more and gratefully move ahead with this offer.

A common occurrence is for journaling to become spiteful, often slamming oneself with mean words, remarkably during the beginning stages of growing a habit. Here, resentments race from the depths like snapping turtles to bite tender toes. However, the time and attention demanded by venting this negativity is wonderful, really, because journaling can relieve tension around emotions and possibly open secure paths to release them.

During this phase, which I know from personal experience can occur over and over throughout a practice, remember your journal is a best friend, and just as can happen with your human friends, your constant caterwauling can bring weariness. Then, overwhelmed with protests, you fall, exhausted from the same one-note energy. This may cause you to lose the inclination to write as it no longer feels safe.

Get unstuck from the unrelenting waves of whining and return to the balance of your practice. This is as simple as equalizing the time you write when you are angry or upset with the time you write when you are happy. If you are not happy at all—which I can tell you I have been there too—focus your words on gratitude. Start and end your journaling session writing down at least five things for which you are grateful. They can seem as mundane as "I am grateful my car cranked, grateful for my comfy shoes, for the sun, for my houseplant, for my heartbeat..." or "I am grateful that I am taking time to write." This not only evens out your writing but also shifts your emphasis to notice things in your life that are well. Good things, even small ones, add up and multiply when gladly noticed, giving you the energy and desire to return to the page the next day.

When I realized I always started my day journaling in the complaint department, I discovered this practice was not only constructing more grievances, but also tainting the flavor of my entire day. I shifted my practice to one more beneficial by writing only gratitude, desires, and positivity in the morning, then returning to my journal at the end of the day to fuss as much as I wanted. After a while, I found I didn't have as many gripes to instigate a tirade because the initial attention on giving thanks brought more gratitude and joy to my day. With the ill will defused, complaints became observations, simply information about things to journal for focus toward resolution and release. I became grateful for this awareness and then even more grateful as I grew.

Ida created a designated "scream document" to vent frustrations. With tension at home as Ida's adult daughter moved back in and clashed with her out-of-work husband, Ida's writing became strained through emotional upheaval and interruptions. Though I suggested she write at her private office, a quiet space overlooking a pond, she bellyached about it being too lonely. My suggestion of trying the library was also sucked into her discord. She had to do it her way, and I respected that. She knew the coast was clear to write whenever her husband was outside in his beloved garden and her daughter was hidden in her room, simultaneously engaged with her dual-screen computer and cellphone. During these times to write, her scream document saw a lot of action as she let the dam burst in a calculated way, writing her frustrations in brightly colored inks. Once the tidal wave subsided, she kept writing and floated into calmer waters, noticing suggestions, creating ideas, and making them her own. With writing safely tucked away, Ida achieved her trusted space to live and journal.

Another occurrence for the journal writer is becoming overwhelmed. Aubrey had a strong urge to write personally for years, but once she sat down and gave herself permission and provided safety, a flash flood of words came much too fast, creating confusion that shut her down. I suggested she safely dip a handful at a time from the torrents that rushed her, using lists, abbreviations, texting language, minimal punctuation, even just one word for each thought until the deluge slowed. Soon, she could get out a phrase, and later, a sentence. After journaling for a couple of weeks, she began to relax, knowing she would show up to journal regularly and there was no need to try to relay everything at once. Her thoughts lined up to express in a more patient, orderly fashion. As Aubrey realized the million miles to the other side comes one squishy step at a time, the stream became manageable.

Other writers get nothing. Zoe said that she would write for about a minute before feeling an intense pain of the valve being shut. She feared the flow of what journaling might reveal. I suggested she revisit this pain, sit with it for an additional minute or two at a time while poised to write, even if she wrote only one word or phrase. If not, make it a quiet introspection with her hands resting on blank paper and a pen. From this perspective, she could reframe the source to allow expression, then forgive and release to safely write again. Just like Aubrey, Zoe had to authorize growth and then trust this practice as meditative, calming, and relaxing before considering undertaking it. Eventually, she cherished it as safe "in her hands."

Even when the words are flowing, sometimes you may notice that your thinking is, well, flat. Stanford lamented his lack of depth and shared, "This isn't exactly what I wrote in my journal, but it was basically 'I loved the musical, the meal was dreadful,' and that was it."

I applauded him for journaling and then offered that our lives can't be captured in a sound bite, a headline, or on a theater's marquee. I suggested if he notices this when journaling and wants to write more, inquire with his thoughts, feelings, and memories around the story like an investigative journalist who forms questions beginning with who, what, when, where, why, and how. Start with the easy questions to establish trusted relationship before leading to the tougher ones to reveal the bigger truth. For example, "Who suggested you go to the show, and why did you love it? What performance or technical aspect wowed you?" as well as "What was dreadful about your dining experience? The food, the ambience, the service? How do you feel about the person who recommended the restaurant? Where else have you dined in the area that you liked, or who could recommend a better place for next time?"

Feel safe to ask questions—writing them in your journal—even if they are asked and not yet answered. And there's no need to review since once you've written the questions, something will stir and surface for you to write...or not. Your journal exposes patterns and passions. Delve into these details. Like feeling a shell in the cove's sand under your feet, it's often what's hidden just beneath the surface that ties your truths together into the complete story or lesson learned. Bring up and examine the shell, judge it if you like, and then treat this plain-looking treasure as a prompt for further writing.

Experiment, remembering there is no wrong way to journal. Slow down and describe the scene in living color, or write in the stream of consciousness, meandering willy-nilly through thoughts and emotions. Gently nudge yourself further by illustrating both the show on stage and the one you are living.

Taste the experience and feel it again. Query your memory in the moment and write the details. Know that this creative expression will happen naturally as you journal.

Writing taps emotions, and journaling allows us to begin our exploration by wading into the waters of our own feelings. I have laughed out loud when journaling, as well as written through sobs where I have gasped for breath, where I've taken my hands off the keys to dry my eyes to see. When I ponder loss, frustration, loneliness, passion, beauty, and dreams, I often cry as if I am seeing a movie about my own life. For this private showing, sometimes closing my eyes makes journaling easier. This occurs through confidence of being in a safe space, a place comparable to a calm, secluded inlet. There lies many colors and emotions between the opposite shores of laughter and tears, and I write my full spectrum.

Intimately discover what safety means and feels like for you in the moment. Float through your consciousness, being vulnerable to the words which come your way, and provide safety for the flow to expand and deepen. Be courageous and champion your strong sensitivity as you journal all of who you are, enhancing your writing spirit. And feel supported each time you breathe.

Fifty years after learning to float, I stood on an empty beach by my rented kayak, assessing the temperament of the ocean's waves. Turbulent for the last few days, I needed to feel safe. My bare shoulders became hot from the midday sun as I looked up and down the beach. Looking out, the waves at the shore broke strong while near the first sand bar, they rolled but looked calm enough. So, I put on my life vest and pulled the kayak in, pushing through the first breaker to hop in and paddle hard to get to quieter waters.

Away from the beach, I relaxed, holding the paddle across my lap as the kayak drifted sideways, parallel with the shore, pointing my vision toward a rogue wave about thirty feet downwind. The instant I turned, one swelled behind me. All I could manage was a couple of swift strokes to point the kayak toward the beach so the wave wouldn't flip me.

The ocean's force swept the boat out from under me, submerging and spinning me around, washing the glasses off my face. Instinctively, I reached out before realizing they were long gone. As I resurfaced and began to find my bearings, a plan to dive ten feet to find the fancy specs sped into my mind, that if only I could get out of the life vest... With fuzzy vision in a tumultuous ocean, I knew my only option was to swim to the beach.

I spotted the kayak five yards in front of me and swam to it, watchful of its erratic movements within the waves. I got my hand on it, pushing it ahead of me and continued this all the way to shore.

Feeling sandy and stupid, I hauled myself and the boat out. As I stood alone in the blistering sun, my condemning thoughts brayed before calming. Other than my pride, I wasn't injured. Yes, my new glasses were gone, but I had an old pair in the beach house. Then I felt Dad's presence, pleased that I was okay and certain I had strengthened my resolve for my own safety with this accident and its lesson.

After fishing out the paddle as it came ashore, I tossed it in the kayak and dragged them up to the dunes. Then I surprised myself by spontaneously whistling a made-up melody as I scuffled with the snaps and ditched the life vest. Grinning with gratitude, I thought about how Dad intuitively knew I was ready to learn to float and swim all those years ago. And I could see how water was the perfect place for me to test self-confidence and grow trust.

I marched back to the sea and fought past that fierce first wave to get in a few feet of water where I fell backwards, having nothing more to lose but the sand off my body. Then, rough as it was, I made peace and floated, playing with the rocky surface, spitting out ocean water, and respecting our relationship while bobbing around like an ice cube. As I trusted I would do with pen in hand later that afternoon, I confidently frolicked in my safety.

4

Safety

Affirming a Journaler's Consciousness

Use affirmations, one or all, adapting as desired.

I know I am safe to write in my journal.

I am vulnerable, facing fears through nurturing self-love as I write.

I revel in authentic sharing, knowing my writing is for my eyes only.

I adopt a soft, loving internal voice for when I encourage myself as I write.

I journal the full spectrum of the colors and emotions in my life.

I champion myself as I write—my frustrations, loneliness, losses, passion, beauty, dreams—anything and everything I am.

I believe being vulnerable brings growth and happiness, so I journal to self-worth and belief in my spirit.

I courageously write whatever comes up, learning not to shut down my expression due to personal judgment or fear.

I balance the time I write when I am angry or sad with the time I write when I am peaceful or happy.

Journaling allows me to enhance the protection of my heart and strengthen my sensitivities.

I relish my relationships, and I support them as I enhance the one I have with myself.

My mind is an inlet for inspiration which flows onto the pages in my journal.

Write an affirmation about securing safety.

o   Begin with either "I am…" or "I…" followed by an action verb in present tense, such as cry, exhale, or march.

o   Complete with heartfelt words to lift your spirit and motivate your growth.

4

Safety

PROMPTING A JOURNALER'S PRACTICE

Choose a word or phrase,
and then journal what comes up.

o Floating

o Being vulnerable

o Vacation

Complete a sentence and write more.

o "Safe places where I would like to journal are…"

o "I enjoy sharing quiet time with…"

o "It happened so suddenly, and the first thoughts that sprang to mind were…"

o "To safely wade into the waters of my feelings, I…"

Create your own prompt and journal from it.

o

5

Writing
Fears

I nurture
positive thoughts
and
empowering beliefs
to propel my
journaling practice.

NEVER MIND
AND THE IDEA EATERS

T he quiet was disarming. Having escaped the sprawl-
ing University of Georgia campus every weekend to
the nourishment and laundry room of my parents'
country home, this was the first Saturday in my tiny room in
a high-rise dorm. After earsplitting Pink Floyd woke me at
dawn, the day turned eerily silent. Many were out of town
with the football team at an away-game while others, like my
roommate, were just away.

I looked out the window at the crystal blue autumn sky,
then turned back to my American History homework. The
subject made my eyes glaze over whether I was listening to
the professor drone on or reading the tedious textbook. As the
afternoon dragged, I sat on my bed, fighting to stay awake...
slumping...losing the battle...

Rapid-fire knocking startled me. My body jerked, and
the book hit the floor, splaying out like a victim primed for
chalking. Focusing, I blinked repeatedly, realizing dusk had
fallen. Soon, it would be dark.

More banging, this time louder and accompanied by a men-
acing grunt. I knew it was Emmett. Yawning, I opened the door.

"Wake up," he said with an impish grin, shaking a thermos. "Gotta get lit for *Night of the Living Dead*."

As he poured antifreeze-green liquid into paper cups, I heard Mom's warning in my head.

Be careful what you drink. Kids get hurt by all kinds of things they think might be fun.

I didn't believe Em would hurt me, but to be safe, I had to ask, "So, what's in it?"

"Zombie repellant!" He cackled like a mad scientist.

"Ah, what's a zombie?"

Though legally an adult at 18, drinking, like zombies, was foreign to me. I had limited exposure to beer and rum, but none to the likes of the undead, much less to their alcoholic antidote.

Seeing me hesitate then sniffing the strange concoction, Emmett spouted, "Don't think. Have fun!"

Don't think? You better overthink each and every risk!

As I worried my spontaneity away, Emmett finished his cup and gave me the stink eye. I returned the gesture while realizing he had already imbibed before he arrived and was still on his feet, so why not?

Walking the half-mile to the makeshift campus theater, Em cheerfully chugged while I cautiously sipped the spiked Kool-Aid, frightened that I might become woozy and fall down. I did my best to listen as he explained the movie's concept of the dead coming back to life, ravenous to eat the living. Upon our arrival, most of the students in the packed house were buzzed, and by his silly laughter, Emmett seemed in synch with everyone else.

Once settled into the desks in the same auditorium where I heard those dull history lectures, that memory vanished when the grainy black and white film began. The movie reminded me of *The Twilight Zone*, a '60s television show I saw via late night reruns in the '70s, one which always scared me as its terror was tough on the screen but then expanded in my imaginative mind.

In the film, siblings Johnny and Barbara visit their father's grave in a country cemetery. When the first zombie appeared, some drunk in the theater screamed, and I jumped. While everyone laughed nervously and opened their flasks, I took a closer look at the zombie. I wasn't sure of its threat; he just looked dirty which explained his bad complexion. Johnny teased his sister that the zombie was coming for her, but she naïvely showed concern for the monster's feelings as he caught and savagely mauled her. Johnny stepped in, and, well, it was downhill from there.

Kids get hurt by all kinds of things...

The injured siblings fled from more zombies, joined others fighting for survival in a farmhouse, and the horror escalated. Like the characters, I had no time to consider what these zombies were or why they acted this way. Between the attacks and securing the house, the eclectic group listened to radio reports from the authorities and media, but details remained sketchy. The phenomenon was a giant mystery that no one could solve. Hearts were ripped out, and minds were forever changed.

Soon, many viewers began to leave. Lumbering toward the exit in various states of drunkenness, these students mirrored the onscreen zombies, their spastic movements distracting and disturbing. I glanced at Emmett looking for comfort but saw his mortified expression as the zombies on screen chowed down.

When the credits rolled, I was very happy to leave, rushing out faster than I would from my history class. However, unlike those egotistical recitations by the blustery prof, I was impacted by the film.

"That was sickening." I shivered, more from fear than the cool air. Struggling to keep up as Em walked with purpose, I asked, "Did you like it?"

He snapped, "It was okay."

On this moonless night as Emmett and I navigated by streetlamps and the occasional automobile's headlights, my once jaunty friend fell silent. He had thought the movie would be sensational, gross-out fun, but it struck a chord, igniting a primal fear.

I ran ahead at one point, placing myself in the dark beyond a circle of light under a streetlamp. I turned, thrusting my arms out, and trudged toward him.

His eyes narrowed as he backed up a couple of steps, raising both fists and voice. "Stop it, or I swear I will hurt you!"

Since he was bigger than me, I didn't push it beyond laughing at him. When I got near him, he hit me anyway, and even though it didn't hurt my upper arm, I acted like it did.

Back in my dorm room, he collected his thermos as I looked in the miniscule closets and under the beds in mock fear, making sure there were no zombies. He wanted me to join him at a party in his dorm across the street, but it was late and I was tired.

"Enjoy yourself," I said, turning down my bed.

Lingering in the doorway, he asked, "Are you okay being here alone?"

I searched his face for clues to why he cared. "Oh! Is what's-his-name throwing the party in your room tonight?"

He fidgeted. "No, he's not there, but there is a party. It's probably going to be too loud to sleep once they get going, and I've got a lot of geology homework to do tomorrow." He intermittently checked over his shoulder. "Do you mind if I stay here?"

I nodded, realizing that my senses were right, and my friend was frightened. "Sure. Go get your toothbrush and stuff."

He paused, thinking, then spat out, "Wanna go with me? We can have a drink before coming back."

One last test. "Nah, you go ahead—"

"Oh, no, that's okay, I'll just crash," he said, slamming the door before plopping down on top of the sheets on my roommate's bed. Apprehensively, he said, "Goodnight."

I bolted the door and turned out the light.

Emmett did not sleep well that night. He was totally freaked. For the first time in our friendship, I saw his panic, and he accepted my help. I discovered that my smart, creative friend had an unusual Achilles' heel. Taking root in his mind, the idea of zombies devoured his sense of normalcy. His fear censored his life. Even though we were safely locked in a tiny room, it didn't matter because the zombies weren't on campus. They were in his head.

As we develop our journaling practice along with an atmosphere of safety, a similar phenomenon happens to all of us. Like the zombies of the George A. Romero film that brought the concept to audiences in 1968, our zombies seemingly appear out of nowhere. As you energize your creativity, encourage growth by opening clear channels, and express yourself fully in your journal, you challenge limiting beliefs. And when you do, the zombies lumber in from the dark depths of your mind to protect their undead survival and parasitic proliferation. Now, it is up to you, and unlike the torches and guns used to combat the zombies in the movie, your only weapons are your wisely chosen words.

When journaling, the insurgents of Never Mind can rise and infiltrate your mind's creative wonderland. Your safety is tested as Never Mind bombards your spirit's steady stream of ideas with worry, anxiety, and doubt. This Legion of Doom strengthens, capturing your precious creativity, using it against you to build up a fighting force of fear, turning inspiration into toxic excuses and unattainable goals. Of course, Never Mind is cunning and devious as its spies, counterintelligence, and double-crossers shapeshift to conform to any situation, thwarting every spark of inspiration. Eventually, you tire and feel the only option is to give up the fight for space to play in this harsh land of negativity.

But do you? Where will your hero come from?

Your hero has been with you all along. Your hero is you! Think about it: Never Mind seems like separation from creativity, but this is not true. Be confident that you are created of creativity to be creative. And creativity is not merely a one-time allowance. Perpetually replenished, it's your choice on how you use this wellspring. You can squander it on private, panicky rants, or you can concentrate it on good.

This tug-of-war with Never Mind happens in consciousness. *Your* consciousness. To clarify, many of us experience doubts within our thoughts. These uncertainties could lead to a mental block which stops you from growing. However, they could also lead to questions, which are prompts, a focus to explore in writing to discover more about yourself and what solutions work for your growth.

There are three levels to your mind. First, you live and express from the conscious mind with awareness of present thoughts, sensations, and perceptions, as well as some memories. Next, the subconscious mind warehouses more memories, ready to call up, while also functioning as the realm of dreams. And finally, the unconscious mind acts similarly to the subconscious, but through your mental conditioning and processes, these life remembrances are locked away from awareness, perhaps due to associated pain, anxiety, or conflict. All three levels affect your thinking, behavior, and creative expression.

If you concede to Never Mind, you become a zombie, suffering in silence, living life mechanically. You are not conscious. You stop acting on your wishes, never utilizing the creative energy you have access to all the time. Only by letting your inspiration go dark does the door close to the light...but the light never goes away.

Know your creativity can still be reclaimed and reanimated. Since you allowed this negative thought to become a belief, affirm a new thought and thus change the effects this thought has in your mind. And a new belief changes your life.

If you remember the issue Never Mind triggers from your conscious or subconscious mind, you can affirm with detail and feeling, thus strengthening your affirmation. If Never Mind's message is true to you without recollection of any previous incident, work with what you have. If you keep affirming from all you know, more of the truth may surface. Even if it doesn't, you're placing a stepping stone on a path to good each time you affirm.

For example, I have heard Never Mind announce this belief in my thoughts:

Journaling is pointless, just a waste of time when there's a dishwasher to empty.

And I lived by this untruth until the day I *really* heard it. I whispered to myself, "Seriously? The dishwasher?!" and then I journaled on this juicy prompt.

Give your worrisome beliefs their own space on the page. Write all the words: the blame, the shame, the guilt, the fears, the incriminating evidence. Write any inside conversations, finger-pointing accusations, or angry altercations thrown at you from Never Mind. Cry if you need to. Howl if it helps. Call a trusted one for support. As much as you can, safely feel the pain, and pour observations, frustrations, and beliefs onto the page.

Next, face this fearful belief head on. Feel what is still real and find the holes in the supposed truth of the story. Take that little entry point and expose the falsehood by writing a new truth for yourself. As Never Mind boisterously berates and issues new charges, begin to feel how the indictments are like a wind to turn against. And know that you do so by making a quick assertion of your newly claimed truth. Even if it's small, it's a little light for your next step to safety.

> I nurture safety in my journaling practice,
> clearing my mind of negative beliefs that try to
> stop me. I write now, and I trust I can put the
> dishes away later.

And the affirmation holds truth to build upon. You are not wishing, hoping, begging, or beseeching; you are claiming your good already received. Begin with a simple and direct "I am" statement:

> I am creative.

You can also use an action verb in present tense. This positive proclamation feels good as you read it or speak it aloud:

I stand in safety as I journal.

And notice how "now" adds a sense of immediacy and an intention toward achievement:

I safely write in my journal now.

You are not waiting for this! Add an exclamation point at the end of the affirmation for emphasis if you like. This is your new truth, your heart's desire, so make it match your enthusiasm for joyful growth.

This affirmation doesn't feel quite right? Know in its initial writing, you are staking your claim which makes space for your positive fulfillment. As you repeat the affirmation, you embolden your longing to live its message. Soon you'll notice signs of this new truth in your options and actions. You may be amazed with these steps in the direction of your good, and you may wonder if they had always been right in front of you. Either way, acknowledge with gratitude, keep affirming, stay alert to forward progress, and grow your beliefs for unlimited creativity and strengthened expression through your journaled words and life choices.

Learn not to fear the fear. Putting your desire into action challenges Never Mind's stance. Journaling and the act of affirming a new truth forces Never Mind's negativity from its stronghold and into the open. Writing down fear's message may not be easy, but it's a step toward understanding that you have accepted these negative ideas as part of your programming. No matter the source, you have adopted them as your own beliefs. Since they are yours, you have the power to change them. So, examine and revise them to suit your growth. Write their opposite. Turn the negative to positive, converting the chatter into conscious intention. Feel the freedom in this new statement, affirm your heartfelt truth, and use your written words for good. Also, build up your resolve as this process is an ongoing one for many who journal, including me.

Never Mind's zombies materialize from a variety of sources, often well meaning, like parents and family members, from neighbors, coworkers, friends, teachers, clergy, politicians, celebrities, the media, advertising…really anyone of any age, living or dead, real or fictitious, human or institution, to whom you opened your mind and accepted their beliefs as your own. Of course, this is how we learn. No matter their intention, other people sharing ideas can reveal a whole new world of possibility and lead to greatness, or they can introduce a zombie into your consciousness, one that will limit your world of thought. Sometimes, for many reasons—age, position, life circumstances, and such—we don't have the discernment to know anything different. We have to grow into this new truth we've accepted, then challenge the lurking, limiting belief once we feel it no longer serves us.

I have realized that no matter their origin, it's not dishonoring to recognize those who planted the seeds of limitation. For instance, over the years, I uncovered a lot of anger around some of these messages taught by my parents, including Nanny, my maternal grandmother who kept me every weekday through childhood when Mom went to the office. Over the years before I started school, she was truly a second mother to me.

Through awareness, journaling, and sharing with trusted ones, I realized that, perhaps more than anyone else in life, parents pass on their beliefs. I opened both my growth path and the relationships once I got to a place of trading blame for forgiveness. I took the realization as practical knowledge, as well as a chance to heal and be grateful to my parents for all their gifts. I loved them, and they loved me. They did everything they could to give me opportunity and support. They passed on beliefs which had benefited them, and some of these benefited me until they just didn't anymore. Other beliefs remain as personal wisdom that I adopted, and I know if they ever need reevaluation, I will recognize this and utilize my tools to shift them.

From a heartfelt caring place, Momma and Nanny overprotected me. My dad was very family-oriented, spending long hours at work to provide for us, and then spending more hours to keep up the home he designed and the land where he built it. He might have welcomed my help if I had shown the desire or aptitude. Recognizing this, he always recommended I help Mom. Later, after we moved to the country when I was a preteen, she would have chores for me and then send me to Nanny's house next door to help her. All of them knew that I was more adept at making a salad or decorating a Christmas tree than using a hammer or pulling weeds. I was happier too.

My mother and grandmother pampered me while also expecting a lot in return, from good grades, which I wanted equally for them and for myself, to my presence, which became smothering to me as a teenager. I loved and emulated them, taking on their language and outlook, including their deep-seated habit of worrying.

I reflected on this habit, journaling about all the bogus collect calls I had to make from childhood into adulthood, lying to the operator to let Mom know I was home safe. On the rare occasion I forgot to call, the phone would soon ring, and I would hear Mom's relief before getting admonished for her having to spend money to find out. Hastily, she'd remind me to be careful and eat well, adding reassurance for whatever was happening in my life, then remind me to come home soon before saying goodbye.

I remembered defending this habit with friends whose parents were more positive about safe arrival while trusting they would be alerted in case of an accident involving their child. I also defended this to myself when I randomly wrote about such worries in my bound journal at night in bed, holding on to the belief that these behaviors were normal, even wise.

As I aged, I learned more of my family's personal stories from times long past and details swept under the rug
ages ago, and then I connected the dots. Best I could tell,
my grandmother, Nanny, was raised by a single mom, likely
amongst addiction and poverty. Then, I heard a few tales of
my grandfather and some stories from their marriage during
the Great Depression and World War II. Nanny raised my
mother with more stability than she had while repeating some
learned behaviors from her own upbringing. After losing her
second child to a congenital heart defect, she was left with
memories of her "blue baby" and a little pride in the big city
newspaper clipping of him being studied by doctors from
around the world. In time, her marriage ended. Later, my
mother mourned her beloved dad when he died at age 42
from cirrhosis of the liver. Mom studied and excelled at the
typewriter and office equipment, working as a trusted secretary in government, legal, industrial, and banking positions
while remaining steadfastly dutiful to her family, including
her mother.

From Dad's stories, most I heard from him as an adult, I
learned his large family farmed in Georgia during the 1920s,
'30s, and '40s. His father was a railroad man before he became
a farmer who engineered enhancements to his tractor, greatly
boosting productivity. He also studied and wrote sermons to
earn ordination as a Baptist minister, serving as an admired
circuit preacher for six small churches. With equal creativity
and talents blossoming in everything his mother set her mind

to do, Granny was the epitome of dedication and nurturance to her family and community. When Dad was barely a teenager, his family faced tragic losses, including the deaths of his father and older brother in less than two years' time, leaving him as the eldest male. His faith provided strength, and he grew into a hard worker who excelled as a mechanical engineer. Trustworthy and well-liked in the corporation where he served for over 30 years, Dad invented machines and secured patents while solving issues at manufacturing plants in the US and abroad. And except for the few times he was out of town, Dad was always at home for supper and in the den reading the paper during family TV time.

Together, Mom and Dad provided a life for me that built on their love and lessons with giant leaps, giving me more options than they had. Even Nanny, in her role as grandmother, had the loving commitment of a second marriage years before my birth. Papa, who immigrated to the US from El Salvador in 1941 for an engineering position, lived morally, valued health, and adored her. With both my grandfathers deceased, he lovingly fulfilled that role for me. Nanny also had my mom, her only child, living next door for the final twenty years of her life. With increased stability, she encouraged me from the best of her heart.

Still, during my upbringing, some of my elders planted seeds that grew into self-doubt from which my perfectionist tendencies created a harsh inner critic. In early adulthood, I noticed how my personal growth was butting heads with some of their direction, so I began to take responsibility and examine my beliefs in relation to their go-to responses. Ultimately, I realized that Mom and Nanny were the most prolific worriers I had ever known, and I finally understood I was too. I mean, really, I was taught by the best.

So, I journaled for years, blaming Mom and Nanny for raising me to worry like them. Then as I lived more of life and began to acknowledge my anxiety and depression, I journaled about how I was the one who had taken their reactions of fear, perfected them as a fixture in my consciousness, and wove them into the fabric of my life. Regarding my maternal influencers, I had to write through my emotions—feelings of anger, loss, acceptance, and forgiveness—as I began to retool those messages and behaviors that I wanted to change for my good.

Unraveling them, I realized my intuitive thoughts were true, that Mom and Nanny saw their actions as protection. They didn't want me to have to experience pain or hardship like they endured. I started to feel their true motive of love. And through many more journaled words and accompanying affirmations as I forgave them, I forgave myself for blaming them, and a little later, for taking on their fears. I even forgave myself for creatively investing in their worried voices, making them my own personal style of repression. I worked to change my habits, affirm new beliefs, and grow self-love. And when I discover stray threads, my journaling practice supports me.

My journaling also shined a brighter light for me to see and embrace all the good Mom and Nanny instilled. I began noticing more and more positive beliefs they planted, calmer words and feelings of nurturance which continued encouraging me. I grew up from their lead, and then I further grew through the journaling process, becoming more compassionate and grateful.

Many years after my journal helped heal my heart, I was surprised that I needed to examine some beliefs from Dad too. We rarely had run-ins as Momma was more present and usually the disciplinarian. Before I entered grade school, I knew Dad was patient, fair, and a good listener. He would deliver his message in a straightforward way, and if I strived to achieve it, we would both be happy. He nurtured me to be whoever I wanted to be as long as I was kind and good. Like Mom and Nanny, he raised me from the best he possessed. But I discovered that my father unknowingly planted a seed in my teen years which sprouted an animosity, one which thrived long into adulthood.

I had just turned 16, and we clashed. Usually, it was Mom and I who would raise voices and have it out; we fluently spoke that highly charged, emotional language. And though Dad didn't raise his voice, his stress was apparent this day when I stood my ground for what I was promised and didn't get: my first car. Honestly, I participated in many high school extracurricular activities, and my parents worked 25 miles away from my school, thus facilitating the need. But yes, I was spoiled, and it wasn't long before I got a car, just not the sassy Pontiac Tempest convertible that he took me to test drive that afternoon.

On our way to see the Tempest, Dad talked about his occasional relationship with the owner, as well as the fact that he knew the fine care he took with his cars. Combined with how we were a loyal Pontiac family, this felt like a done deal. Seeing the Tempest, top down, not even an oily smudge on the engine—Perfect!—I was smitten. As my fantasies of driving it in the homecoming parade and being the coolest kid at my not-so-cool rural school, Dad held all his cards from view, congenial with the man as they talked mechanics, mileage, and money.

On the outset of our twenty-minute drive back home, he casually dismissed my excitement, sharing he had no intention to purchase the car before we drove across the county to see it.

My anger boiled up, but my mother had conditioned me to never raise my voice with my father, telling me when I was very young that doing so would "kill him." Unlike Mom and I, Dad really didn't like to argue, something I noticed early on and again as I aged when I realized he and Mom never seemed to have disagreements. Also, I'm sure Mom didn't mean her statement literally. Still, this was a tough thing for a sensitive kid to carry.

Riding in Dad's truck that day, I retreated far inside myself, and once home, I fled to my bedroom to stew. I put on some records, but hearing music didn't help, so I turned them off. Then, even with a bed and a chair to sit on, I stiffly stood and began to blast my feelings onto the page. When Dad knocked on the door asking to talk, I refused, saying I was writing. This was honest but also manipulative since with writing, like homework, I knew he would leave me alone.

The real sassy tempest was me, now hiding out on the floor on the far side of the bed with a notebook and pen, fueling my rage into what became a poem, a genre in which I never wrote. The cadence and rhyme seemed to satisfy my victimhood. Then, finished and pen down, I slumped over and cried.

After being sullen at supper and recoiling in my room until everyone was in bed, I quietly crept the long hallway to the kitchen for some tea, pouring by the light of the fridge.

As I started back to my hideaway, passing by the darkened den, I heard, "Son?"

I stood in the arched entrance to the unlit room, too ashamed to walk in and too nervous not to be in a position where I could bolt if needed, especially if I began to cry. I mumbled, "Yessir."

He said that he wanted to talk to help me understand his side of the story. Though he didn't voice an apology, his tone was peaceful, and my heart opened. From my crabby mood, I told him I understood.

Then he said, "If something like this happens again, don't write about it. Talk to me."

I instantly felt scolded, furious, and further shut down because I liked to write. More than that, I also felt ashamed that I had hidden from him on the page, like I hadn't "honored thy father." These feelings became beliefs, and for years, this hindered me from writing to that depth when I felt angry, sad, or depressed, any emotion that wasn't happy, kind, good... or appropriate.

So, many years after journaling and changing beliefs adopted from Mom and Nanny, this incident with Dad came up out of the blue during a personal growth workshop. With perspective, I knew I had avoided Dad that afternoon, but being with myself and my writing was the best I could do at the time. As I realized his stinging reprimand was more of a request, I affirmed how much good had come from my journaling to help me understand what happened and how to mend fences both inside and outside of self. Then more anger surfaced, and I was furious at him all over again. I wrote about it as I felt the feelings, writing my viewpoints from every angle. I put them in perspective of our current relationship and the time that had passed, and I set an intention to forgive him. I wrote on this topic whenever it appeared, journaling every little nuance, sometimes returning to the page to add more that day. I wrote any thought or detail to keep the door open and not sweep it under the rug like I did when sulking as a teen.

Through the weeks and more journaling, as well as frequently using the affirmations which came from it, I realized that what Dad said about my writing wasn't meant to keep me from a gift that enhanced my life and brought serenity. He was simply saying that he wanted to be with me and help me through my anger. I knew that the condemnation I felt wasn't his intention as he always encouraged me, even when he himself hadn't experienced what I was going through. He needed to both be heard and to hear me, and he didn't understand that I could say no more until I was clear. It probably seemed odd to him—it was even weird to me—that I could articulate so much, yet sometimes I found feelings I couldn't verbalize. I was afraid of my own anger, especially around him, and journaling allowed me a path to understand how to honor and interact with my emotions.

Through my private writing, I grasped what a glorious gift Dad had given me. I don't know that I could have learned such a profound lesson to empower my journaling any other way. I felt grateful to him as my teacher and to myself for exploring the depths, learning the lesson, and moving forward to live more fully with my practice. Claiming my writing as a positive force in my life boosted my self-esteem while it also rounded out the forgiveness I gave Dad and myself.

My growth was most often realized privately through journaling and reflection. Like the initial hiding of the issue, the process of pulling back and cleaning out from under the proverbial rug had to be behind closed doors; it was the only way that felt safe to me. Years later through my trusted ones—cherished friends and counselors—I built the courage and learned the language to maintain safety in certain circumstances and get guidance from others.

I never spoke directly to Dad about the tempestuous issue from days gone by, but after moving in with him and Mom for a short time during the divorce in my late forties, he respected my writing time. For years, I had shared about my journaling practice, and he knew it was a lifeline. Then through his remaining years, the growth from my journaling supported me to open up to him about my challenges, beliefs, and triumphs. And more than ever, he shared his heartfelt stories with me, even some of his tears. Learning more about the times he lived in, as well as the options he had to choose from, shifted my perspective on how different his early years were from my own. These exchanges also demonstrated that when I was happy, kind, and loving when I spoke to myself, it enhanced my doing so with others. My safety deepened.

I have spent many hours and many pages pondering where my Never Mind's messages originated. While some were evident, others took more time, space, and maturity for retrieval.

And even with cultivated safety and the process in place, others remain mysteries. For those messages whose origin was still unknown, I gave up the search. It no longer mattered who shared them. The truth is I accepted these messages, so

I could recognize these blocks, claim them as my own, and take responsibility for changing them by affirming a positive belief through my journaling practice.

It's good to remember that, just like me and everyone else, you are unique in your choices of how to live and express yourself. These messages may have suited you well at some point, or you would have never accepted their resonance into your consciousness. Others may have been so prevalent that you didn't question them. Perhaps you didn't have a choice, and these beliefs were impressed upon your will. At some point later—like the 25 years that lapsed between me, my dad, and the test-driven Tempest—you find the safety to be aware of them when they emerge. The time is right, and it's never too late. The immediate go-to emotion has softened, and you can see the limiting belief in a new light to survey its message. Now, you have the chance to grow as you shift your thinking. With your new thought, begin to bring creativity back to the light of your life. Journal a path to forgive others and yourself, see the gift from your journey, and instill a smart, heartfelt belief to live by.

I reflected on this while conducting a journaling workshop for teens where I encountered a boy with multiple piercings and slick black hair covering his eyes Emo-style. When I asked him about his writing experience, he upturned his head toward me. I imagined he was peering through the sheepdog-like locks that hung to the tip of his nose.

Soft-spoken and well mannered, he responded, "I like to write, but I'm a bad writer."

"Do you ever write just for yourself?" I asked.

He shook his head.

I suggested he examine his current belief and change his thinking, so he could exercise his desire and accept the goodness in his journaling, maybe even feel he's a good writer.

The mop of hair moved from side to side as he shook his head again before turning away. I thought of how some zombie chastised him for either what he wrote or the act of writing itself, and the intimidated teen believed the zombie was right. I picked up his pen, handed it to him, touched the notebook gently, and said, "Would you please give it a try?" He tilted his head down, the screen of hair falling upon the paper like a curtain onto a stage.

When I came round a few minutes later, I asked him how it was going. Without a word, and perhaps without an expression or eye contact, he handed me the paper. On it was scrawled, "I want to write more." He wasn't ready to say he was a good writer, but he'd faced his issue and affirmed his desire to journal.

I placed the paper on his desk. "Very good. Believe it and keep writing."

Thinking outside the box expands the box, giving you wiggle room. This small sense of freedom prepares you to open the box to your widespread creativity in this step-by-step journey of growing self-trust. Affirmations build up conscious reinforcements for positive change, eventually adding under-pinnings for mounting new beliefs in the subconscious. As you doubt the doubt, hassle the worry, unnerve the anxiety, interrogate the fear, and negate the negativity, Never Mind reveals its hand, the one that's been directing the show in your mind. Then write a positive truth and repeatedly return to this written record of affirmation for strength, knowing new beliefs are being reinforced.

And since we are writing for a period of time without reading our journals, consider copying these affirmations into another notebook or computer document—an affirmation journal—so you can easily use them now. Remember your affirmations may sound and feel silly because there's part of you that stubbornly believes the old truth and fearfully resists change. Remain assured in your beliefs and brave in your actions to realize your new desire. Follow your creativity to develop a system that enhances your good.

For me, the moniker "Never Mind" personifies these negative beliefs. Having a name also separates these views from those thoughts which serve me well. Early in life, I experienced Never Mind's voice directed at me in second person, most often sounding like Mom or Nanny. Later, it also presented in first person as my moody teen self. Building my journaling habit switched it up.

Upon solidifying my practice, affirmations held a majority of time in the first person, internal voice which echoed the positive "I am" statements. Never Mind retreated to second person and shifted predominantly to my teen voice, even if the old belief was learned from a parent or authority figure. Now, Never Mind's taunts and outdated beliefs are regularly examined and amended to affirmations, sometimes in my journal but also on the spot in thought. This process continually guides me to own and nurture my voice, both the one I speak, as well as the one I hear in my thoughts.

Being playful empowers creativity, so use your imagination to hear, picture, and characterize your version of Never Mind. Make it personal to strengthen the image and the feeling, so you easily recognize it and utilize it in your practice. For instance, zombies work for some, but I have also coached journalers who experience them as similarly violent figures like snipers or terrorists. One woman envisioned hers as The Committee, like a supreme court so high up on a bench that all she saw was the wall and all she heard were their voices raining down severe verdicts against her journaling. Some have only a singular entity, visualizing them as Guard Dog, Silencer, Evil Eye, or My Bully. Others deal best with the concept by making it comical, like a young woman who visualized her journaler's consciousness housed in the most popular discotheque in town. All her freedom and creativity danced inside under the spinning mirror ball, but she could rarely maneuver past the velvet rope and its vain, judgmental Doorman.

Whatever you call it and however you cast the role, Never Mind is not some giant mystery you can't solve. This nemesis seemingly cages your creative expression while really offering an opportunity to reclaim it through your journey. When you stand in your fear, your creativity hasn't been seized; you've willingly submitted to self-oppression. You must confront the enemy inside—your belief in your fear—to stand in your power and recover your creativity. You don't need to naïvely show concern for Never Mind's feelings; they are thoughts in your head, thoughts to be changed for your creative revival and growth. Move beyond victimhood. Be breathtakingly honest and assert a new belief for yourself. Don't ask; affirm, believe, and receive. Align with your confidence in creativity, and use present-oriented, first person statements in relatable words to imagine, enact, and then live this truth. Establish safety, then playfully celebrate your aliveness through your journaling.

For Emmett, zombies continued to roam his consciousness some thirty years later. On a winter trip to Florida's panhandle, walking the deserted Mexico Beach in broad daylight, he mentioned a new movie he wanted to see: *Zombie Strippers*. After nonchalantly rolling my eyes, I pulled the trick of mimicking a zombie.

He stopped in his tracks and puffed up, responding as he had many years before. "I'll hurt you! I will!"

This time we both laughed, came together grinning, and bumped shoulders to continue our stroll. Safe, we trusted we would never hurt one another.

Em found twisted thrills out of feeding on those gory movies, realizing that both creative state and zombie state were inside jobs of interpreting outside influences. He got a kick out of dancing on the precipice of his fear, experiencing the rush, yet he knew at any time he could make the conscious choice of when to look at the free-for-all or when to look away at something freeing.

In every area of your life, you always have choices. To write, choose a positive affirmation, empower yourself, and then go to your journal.

And in your life story, you are the hero, right?

Good! Now, write your heart out.

5

Fears

AFFIRMING A JOURNALER'S CONSCIOUSNESS

Use affirmations, one or all, adapting as desired.

I write my limiting beliefs, celebrating the awareness they signal as I create a new, affirmative belief.

I reclaim power taken by fear and use it to change my thinking and propel my writing.

I affirm a positive truth and receive good in my journaling practice. I give thanks!

My Never Mind is built from beliefs shared by a variety of sources. As I consider the origin, I trade blame for forgiveness.

My affirmations stake the claim, making space for creative fulfillment, and through repetition, living its purpose and lifting my writing spirit.

I no longer permit fears to steal my inspiration, darken my imagination, and work against my journal writing.

I welcomed and nourished my negative belief. Now, I change it, making it positive for my next steps to journal.

I am grateful that I am in charge of my thinking, my choices, and my writing.

I release my fear of the fear, giving credit to affirmations and my journaling practice.

I trust that even if the door is closed to the light, the light never goes away. Through positive belief, I write and let in the light.

Creativity is always with me, supporting my journaling.

I am my own hero. I empower myself in my journaling practice now.

Write an affirmation about overcoming fears.

- o Begin with either "I am…" or "I…" followed by an action verb in present tense, such as seize, assert, or shapeshift.
- o Complete with heartfelt words to lift your spirit and motivate your growth.

5

Fears

PROMPTING A JOURNALER'S PRACTICE

Choose a word or phrase,
and then journal what comes up.

o   Wonderland

o   Something swept under the rug

Complete a sentence and write more.

o   "I hear my Never Mind, and it says…"

o   "As I journal, I am most afraid of…"

o   "I feel free when…"

Create your own prompt and journal from it.

o

6

Writing
Awareness

I am
energized
to discover
and journal the
plentiful details
of my life.

Now, The Sensual Now

I kept beat to Cher wailing "Half Breed," rhythmically running my toes through my bedroom's shag carpeting, completely ignoring the ninth-grade term paper I had to write. Exasperated at Momma vacuuming up and down the hall, I focused on my tropical fish frolicking in the bubbles to the song's tribal drums and screeching violins while I killed time until eight o'clock when I would start watching three solid hours of television.

Now in the spare bedroom across the hall, Mom's Eureka won the battle for airwave supremacy as Cher's song faded to a close. As the needle lifted off the record and moved away in time for the next 45 to drop, Mom continued, no doubt moving on to the painstaking task of attacking the baseboards with the hose attachment. The opening guitar riffs of Elton John's "Saturday Night's Alright for Fighting" blasted, and I bounced on my springy bed as his band joined in before he began singing.

Without warning, Elton's voice slurred to a halt. The bubbles quit churning in the tank. My mother's vacuum whirred down to silence, and after I heard her click the power switch twice, she shouted, "Honey!"

From the kitchen on the far end of the house, Dad yelled, "I'll check the breakers!"

I hopped up and went to my window to scan the sky. The hardwood trees that bordered the lawn stood motionless, their lush green leaves speckled by autumn's yellow and orange. No clouds above, so the usual electrical storm didn't make this happen. There wasn't even a bird flying within the forty yards between our house and the unstriped, rural road with the cotton field on the other side.

I went to the kitchen where Mom stood, hands on hips, surveying Dad's aborted task: half the dishes unrinsed and unready for the dishwasher. And even though it wasn't dripping, she tightened the faucet's knobs to satisfy her concern that what was left in the lines remained since our well's electric pump couldn't do its job. Humming, Dad came in from the utility room holding a dishrag.

"Why's the power out?" I asked.

Dad folded the rag as he leaned against the counter. "A transformer could've blown."

Not surprisingly, Momma had an opinion. "Well, it could be—"

Like a TV sitcom, Nanny, my mom's mom who lived next door on our seven acres, made an entrance through the carport door without knocking.

I walked over and hugged her. "Power's out."

"What, Sugar?"

Mom added, "Yep. Electricity went dead a few minutes ago."

"Well, goodness," Nanny said, cruising the countertops. "I was just out looking for Papa in the garden and thought I'd see if you had any homemade biscuits left from supper."

"Nope," Momma stated. "Daddy made a pan of cornbread while I vacuumed the house. He got supper ready so quick that we ate, and then I tried to finish vacuuming, but the power died."

"I wish I could still vacuum," Nanny said, rubbing her elbows, "but with my arthritis…"

I averted my gaze, hoping she wouldn't enlist me, but I caught Momma's eyes on the way to getting mine focused on the floor. Her casting shame burned into me.

"Well…" Nanny froze, letting that word hang in the air, empty of any possibility of cleaning help or leftover biscuits, "…that's a deep subject."

Looking up at Nanny, I said, "When the power's on, I'll come and vacuum for you."

Nanny reacted as if I had just given her a bouquet. "Oh, that's sweet, but don't you have homework?"

"Yes, ma'am," I said, and then glanced at Mom. "I'll get it done before then."

Nanny pulled a Salem out of her worn cigarette case and turned to the door. "As long as you do your homework."

"Mother, it might be a while before we get power," Mom said. "This could be bad. Someone could have wrecked into a power pole like that high school girl did when she was driving drunk. Ran off the road and wrapped her car around that power pole, or she would've landed in the creek. Would've died either way. And the power was out all night and half the next day." Sighing, she added, "The things kids do…"

As Nanny went out the door, pausing to light up before closing it, I grabbed my Tupperware tumbler and headed to the fridge.

Momma quickly blocked my path. "What do you want?"

"Some more iced tea."

"Well, you can't leave the refrigerator open too long, or the food will spoil," Momma said without budging. "We don't know when we'll have power again."

"I'm thirsty now." I locked eyes with her and shook the remaining nuggets of ice in the bottom of the plastic cup. To break the standoff, I added an obligatory, "Please."

She exhaled before quickly opening the door to grab the pitcher, simultaneously sitting it on the butcher block as she shut the door tightly. "Now. There."

I poured some, then looked back at her. "Can I get some ice?"

"No, it's already cold," she snapped, moving the pitcher to the cabinet next to the fridge. "Why don't you go do your homework?"

"Because," I said flatly, "I don't have any light."

"Sit by your window or go out on the patio," Mom said.

"But it's getting dark. And there are mosquitoes," I protested.

"You could use a kerosene lamp," Dad suggested, "just like I used on the farm when I was your age."

Dreading another tale about the good ole days, I looked in the tumbler, wishing I could drown. Unlike the rest of us, it seemed his family always rose before dawn in South Georgia, fed the cows and chickens, toiled in the hot sun one day, then walked to school through the blinding snows the next. They fell asleep when it got dark because "dawn came early." He said people knew each other better back then. Well, maybe, but they didn't know Cher.

"Or you can use a candle," Mom offered, "but you've got to be careful not to set the house on fire."

"No thanks," I said as I left. Feeling my way down the windowless, paneled hall to my bedroom, I heard them discuss the location of batteries and how they should be preserved in case we needed to hear emergency broadcasts as if war had broken out.

I got to my room, started to shut the door but stopped, feeling frightened of the looming darkness. The phone rang, startling me until I remembered that it worked whether or not the power was on, and I heard Momma in the kitchen talking to Nanny. Yes, she said, we are saving water from the shared well and being careful with candles. No, she didn't know if she'd cook biscuits, if anything, tomorrow since the house was total electric. She said goodbye, and I heard her hang up the receiver.

Then all was quiet as dusk fell. I climbed into bed and stared at the outline of my record player with 45s still stacked up, knowing "Boogie Woogie Bugle Boy" was up next. My thoughts swung to a reminiscence of a bright afternoon a week ago. That peppy tune played, and I couldn't help but bop around.

Mom popped her head in, asking, "Where did you get that record?"

Unsure of why she cared, I answered that I had traded for it with a friend.

"Is that the Andrews Sisters?"

I told her it was Bette Midler.

She shrugged and shared, "It sure sounds like them. You know, I used to jitterbug to that song when I wasn't much older than you. Want me to show you how?"

I nodded, and she put the clothes basket on the bed and walked over, taking my hands. She taught me the basic steps before the song ended. Playing it a few more times, we danced and giggled. She gloated about how dance partners would wildly spin her around and throw her into the air, and I could sense how much she loved that. Then, the 45 ended, and I didn't catch the needle before it moved aside, and another record dropped. She picked up the basket, winked at me, and walked out before the next song began to play.

After my smile faded from the memory, I sat there for what seemed like an eternity until I was spooked by a splashing sound when a fish broke the water's surface.

Once in a while, I would hear a car's loud muffler on the road but other than that, with few neighbors yet abundant fields and woods, not a sound. My hearing struggled to find some noise to make itself useful. It was like the apocalypse had happened, and we were just on the edge of devastation, too far out to see the smoke, hear the sirens, or smell the burning mass destruction, probably the fault of some kid burning a candle.

My mind strayed to how boring it must have been to live on a farm like Dad in his family of eight, then I realized I was in similar circumstances in the boonies without power and water. So, what good was air conditioning, indoor plumbing, and electrical appliances? Okay, I did have my own room and bath whereas, as far as I knew, his large family lived in a cozy house. I imagined it was very clean, smelling of line-dried linens, food fresh from the garden, and baked sweets from heaven, thanks to my Granny. Dad rarely elaborated on these details, only the rural road where the house was located, sometimes its acreage, and usually the crops they cultivated, the poisonous snakes they killed, and the juiciest tomatoes they savored.

As night fell and I snuggled into my soft bed, I heard someone shuffling down the carpeted hallway, and then I saw a beam of light jostling around like it was struggling to escape. Dad popped in and tossed the flashlight next to me.

"May as well go to sleep. Nothing's gonna get ya," he reassured me for the gajillionth time in my thirteen years of fear of the dark. "Goodnight."

"'Night," I said. I knew he was right, but my worried imagination fought it anyway.

Oh, sure, he won't hear any ruckus in the night over his snoring, but he will see the gruesome scene when dawn comes. Pffft.

Once he closed their bedroom door, my eardrums succumbed to the quiet. The air was becoming stale without circulation. My mouth tasted bitter from supper's fried okra and cheesy tuna casserole, and the aroma was entering my sinuses. I got up and navigated with flashlight and dilated pupils to the bathroom. After brushing my teeth, using only a sip of water, I put the lighted end of the flashlight in my mouth and looked in the mirror at my horrible reflection. Then I cut off the flashlight, letting my eyes adjust. I stared outside, safe with the window between me and Bigfoot, who would most certainly cross the huge yard at any moment in the shadows cast through the trees by the obscured moon. Without drawing the drapes, I crawled into bed, looking at my watch with the phosphorescent dots next to the numbers. It was barely after eight, and I'm missing Mary Tyler Moore, Bob Newhart, and Carol Burnett.

Quickly, I fell into a deep sleep, dreaming of Daddy burning carpet scraps after we moved in. I saw them ignite and melt straightaway, spewing a dense, toxic cloud. Momma, from somewhere, warned me to stand back, and I floated off to a safe, quiet place so far away that I jerked myself awake when every light in the room illuminated, the aquarium pump spat and hissed, and Elton John whirred back into song. Miffed, I got up, silenced Elton, primed the pump, closed the drapes, and turned off the lights.

Anytime—except from a sound sleep in the wee hours of the morning—waking to our full sensual experience is an inspiring gift to illuminate our life and spark creativity. And to satisfy a desire for more vivid expression, we sharpen our awareness in our journals. With practiced awareness, we reflect in words both what we receive from the world and what we reflect back.

Awareness happens in the Now. From outer and inner perception on nine levels, awareness is realized through the:

Physical senses of hearing, seeing, smelling, tasting, and touching

Emotional sense of feeling

Mental senses of thinking and knowing

Subconscious sense of intuiting.

Both the past and the future also happen in the Now. Yes, even when remembering what was or imagining what might be, the action occurs in your current point of view. Also, be aware of spinning in thoughts of worry, doubt, and anxiousness as Never Mind pulls you into negativity of the past and fear of the future, robbing you of present possibilities. Choose to use your awareness to remain positive.

As I remembered and wrote the story above, I experienced all five physical senses. I saw and heard the bubbling aquarium, the record player blasting the sounds of Elton John and Cher, as well as the absence of sound in the still trees and silent house. I felt the touch of the soft carpeting on the pads of my feet. The bitterness of after-dinner breath overtook my nose and mouth, apparent through smell and taste.

Mentally, I knew that an electrical storm, the common culprit for a rural power outage, wasn't the cause. I understood Mom was providing another public service announcement about the dangers of driving drunk while Nanny was once again hunting Mom's treasured biscuits. I thought it wise to end the stalemate with Mom at the fridge by being polite, even though my heart wasn't in it. I also knew that Dad was about to go down memory lane and repeat an oft told tale from his boyhood.

This played into my emotions as I felt I wouldn't enjoy hearing a repeat of one of his stories. I also experienced fear of the dark, plus my intuition knew that Dad was correct about my safety, even if Never Mind denied it.

Akin to inspiration's creative spark which ignites imagination, intuition feels natural yet beyond conscious thought. Delivered to mind from the subconscious, it seems similar to a nighttime dream. Perhaps at other times, intuition feels ethereal, rising like an instinct or primal warning from the unconscious mind. Intuition can also be revealed through a unique awareness from other senses. Some believe these messages are the heart speaking while others feel intuition is otherworldly.

To broaden awareness in both my life and journal, I wrote examples of the nine senses daily. I honed my perceptions with instances in the present or from the previous 24 hours while also practicing journaling skills. The more I did this, the more my senses enhanced my written words.

This focus allows you to fully experience each precious moment instead of killing time by living unaware. So, make a list of the five physical senses along with the emotional, mental, and subconscious senses, then use these as prompts to catalog a quick example of each in your journal. Even if just an ordinary day, this choice boosts awareness of your senses, your thoughts, your feelings, and your guidance.

Consider how vacation stimulates alertness. Paris was an infinite buffet for every level of my senses, and I consumed as much as I could, journaling about it each day of the week. This alertness holds true even if I've traveled somewhere multiple times. I think of the beaches I have visited over and over again. I feel equally excited for what's new and what's the same. Upon arrival, I roll down the car windows and inhale the salty air. Sometimes I whiff nasty wharf smells, but it doesn't matter as it's part of the character of the vacation spot. It's too fresh to be irritating. Just as awareness soars in a spectacular new locale or a favored spot to visit, it also brings out the extraordinary in the commonplace.

Your senses are heightened when you go through something incredibly touching or traumatic. Consider the details you remember of a baby's birth or a loved one's passing; of being caught off guard by friends at your surprise birthday party or catching your finger in a closing cabinet door; of happening upon something special you thought you'd never see again or of being pulled on stage at an improvisation performance when your stomach was already nervous. Every sense on every level was elevated. Nothing else mattered because of your laser-honed focus on the Now.

After intensifying your senses, amplify your awareness by writing them in your journal. Rise above the action to observe it as you write about what happened to you, with you, about you, and around you. Zoom out and zoom in to be authentic in capturing both big picture and fine detail. Create the full panorama of sensations, emotions, thoughts, and insights. Treat observation as a meditation of awareness as you challenge yourself to journal the whole truth.

Be sure to play! Journal your colorful visualizations and scattershot daydreams as they are as alive in the present moment as your free-flowing writing. A fun way to increase awareness is to remember how, as kids, we were often over-the-moon excited with all the possibilities.

When I was little, I played make-believe as Robin to an imaginary Batman, as well as a pioneer, a game show emcee, a castaway, or a dog running in a pack beside my family's beloved mutt Princess. I imagined myself as a doctor, butterfly, space alien, or soap opera star. I played king of the world as easily as an orphaned street urchin. I could pick up a stick and imagine it as a pirate's sword for swashbuckling or a baton leading the parade band. With an extra stick, I could extend my arms and have huge wings like a pterodactyl. On my bike, I was a racecar driver or a jockey in the Derby.

Playing these games brought giddiness. My little body tingled. I loved that rush of electricity, that feeling I now know as pure creativity pulsing through me. Instinctively, I knew my talent for play and storytelling, and I easily put passion and time into creation.

Momma often told me to "go outside and play." Sure, this time to make up games and amuse myself got me out from under her feet, but it was truly for my own good. In the fresh air and sunshine in our fenced backyard—and later, with permission, by bike all over the neighborhood—I played and played, accepting more inspiration, making the most fun creative choices, and extending the reach of my imagination.

On our own, we are responsible for taking care of ourselves. Similar to a child asking for what's desired to spur the ensuing gifts from Santa Claus, we have to be our own parent. And in a journaling practice, we expand our meaning of "gifts" to include more intangibles to enrich our often-busy lives. Remember, created of creativity to be creative? We were born innately creative, and this precious gift not only lives within us, but when nurtured, our capacity to receive grows along with us, no matter our age. So sometimes, we must schedule spontaneity and be intentional to nurture our full sensory awareness in the Now.

Throw yourself a Me Party! Take your journal and get outside your usual day-to-day. Be in the moment to playfully stoke the flame and fire up your awareness. Go alone, if possible. Unplug. No screens, no constraints. Relish the freedom. Since time may fly while you're having fun, set a timer for your return, if needed, but resist checking it. Do your thing and trust the timer to do its thing.

Stress and anxiety may come up but can be relieved as you invoke and emulate your inner child. This is *your* time to go outside and play! Being childlike and welcoming of creativity within the splendor of the moment's details brings wonder and magic. Notice both the enormous and miniscule insights caught by your physical, emotional, mental, and intuitive senses. And then realize you aren't seeking to find inspiration outside of you; you remain aware of the inspiration suddenly igniting *inside* of you. Simply surrender to the parade of light-filled visions, recognize the ideas that spark through your senses, then make a choice—That one!—and run with it on the ready-and-willing page of your journal.

I took my journal to an arts center I had never visited, drawn to an exhibit by a painter who depicted scenes of childhood birthday parties on large canvases. After my first respectful glance at the paintings, hands clasping my journal behind my back, my inner child took over. I felt lighter, excited, and compelled to journal. I wrote standing in the middle of the gallery but had a wild urge to sit on the floor. Even though I was mostly alone, Never Mind butted in on my bliss.

What will people think? I'll get kicked out and be humiliated!

I listened, realizing Never Mind's negativity was the opposite of my inner child's urge to explore and create, which I was venturing to enhance during this Me Party. I jotted the worried warning in my notebook then plopped down on the polished hardwoods and kicked off my clogs. After defiantly writing an affirmation to declare opposition to Never Mind's message, I glanced at the paintings, felt a smile rise on my face, and continued to journal the thoughts and feelings each painting brought up for me. I soaked in the joy of journaling away from my desk, jubilant as I wrote my private thoughts in a public space. Truly, I had gone outside and was playing! The more I wrote, the more I was delivered. And when I had spent enough time with a painting, I scooted on my fanny to be in front of the next one.

Walking back to my car, Never Mind condemned the experience.

How was driving across town to journal beneficial? You know there's work on the desk, the garden to water, and a meal to cook. What a waste of time!

I was buzzing, all aglow from my time well spent, and yet that voice in my head tried to bring me down. I confidently acknowledged Never Mind's message as I got into my car. Opening my journal, I answered my censor by writing on the feeling of accomplishment, of being aware and alive in the moment, and then dismissed the hostility.

I also journaled to affirm a wonderful coincidence of seemingly unrelated events happening together as a direct response to my thoughts. Now, I trust that what I think, want, and believe stimulates my reality, and this can include both good and bad. Some thoughts are cancelled out by others while other thoughts may take a while to come to life. Some of these manifestations are evident very quickly when I am aware of my outer and inner worlds, and those occurrences are very present and, even if perceived negatively, still quite magical. To experience this, I have to be alert while simultaneously aware of intuitive guidance from within.

For instance, when I arrived at the arts center, I was skeptical of the process. Walking up the steps to the entrance, I stopped and jotted a journal entry, wondering if I should really be there. Unbeknownst to me, a children's performance was ending inside an interior room just out of view. The moment I stepped over the threshold, an eruption of enthusiastic applause greeted me. Alone, I stopped and took it in as an evocative reply to my curiosity. What a wildly creative answer and also a big welcome. And while standing in the doorway, I journaled my full awareness.

And somehow I knew the experience would be good for me; this came through an instantaneous gut feeling when I saw the brief description of the painting exhibit. Involuntarily, intuition is often an internal voice that can provide guidance. Though somewhat mysterious and unexplainable, intuition arrives like inspiration.

For me, intuitive thought differs from those of Never Mind, which when heard and felt are often cross, critical, and manipulative. Intuition is positive, encouraging me to explore, change, and grow, to be fully alive. At other times, the messages of intuition and Never Mind might sound the same. For example, Never Mind can mimic the serene voice of intuition to hijack blossoming creativity. In this case, I pay close attention to the meaning of the tranquilly delivered words, coaxing me toward the dimming light of laziness, the dense fog of inertia, or the action of doing something other than being creative. This led me to trust the feeling that accompanies intuition's guidance, even receiving the message through a feeling.

And though the arts center was open to the public, Never Mind sensed my uneasiness and portrayed multiple roles through the usual players, providing endless reasons to leave. These included both the first person "I" front and center, criticizing myself, as well as the second person "you" aiming attacks from offstage. Upon hearing these fraudulent understudies, I used tools to obstruct my internal irritant once again, reclaiming my creativity and centering my consciousness.

Practice your awareness skills by getting outside your world with a Me Party. So, where to go? Be playful! Take a cue from the weather, and if you love the rain, get out in a summer shower with the purpose of playing in puddles then journaling under an umbrella. Ruminate on the fun of Halloween when you give yourself permission to imitate someone else. Put on a wig or a mustache with a hat and sunglasses, some sort of passable disguise, then grab your journal and head to a shopping district or park. Find a bench where you can write incognito in the midst of activity. Take hints from recurring symbols in your nightly dreams, where, if you love to dream of flying, go ziplining, writing observations on the aerial platform in the trees between lines. Wherever you go, be safe, feel free, and write on your special experience.

You don't have to travel far or even spend money. My arts center visit was nearby and free. Go to a tourist site or a walkable neighborhood with interesting houses, any place that has drawing power for you. As fantastic as Paris was for me, there are shopping centers in my city focused on the cultures of Asia, as well as those of Central and South America, where most products, signage, and speech are unfamiliar to me. This rich experience completely changes my perspective as it's like being in a foreign land though only a few miles from my home. It also proves that a smile is universal communication as I interact with others and take in the atmospheric details. I enjoy shopping with a couple of bucks to buy something, then experience it. For example, I brewed tea I had bought, and while it steeped, I noticed color, steam, and aroma as I journaled the sensational experience. When I sipped and winced at the bitter taste, I added honey, but one of the sweetest, most sensual foods in the world couldn't compete with the bite. No loss there, only gains with all the more to journal.

Even when focused on a usual day, open your mind and heart to release the need to know details before you venture to discover them. Stay open to the originality of the moment.

Take your journal to a theater to watch a film you know nothing about. Sink into the experience, writing details and feelings by the light of the screen. Consider, we often study something from afar instead of leaning in and living it, and this is a trap; let your awareness lead you to action and interaction.

Don't overthink. Have fun! Be smart, but don't overanalyze, thus missing out on the real deal. And feel bountiful in energy and abundant in your writing. Get in the habit of being fully present as participant and observer all the time, and then journal, whether centered by a prompt or flying footloose and fancy-free, to go wherever your practice takes you.

Sitting on my bed in the dark, quiet house with only a sliver of the moon for light, I was forced to deal with my immediate circumstances, viewed my home as never before, and caught my first conscious glimpse of what it is like to be fully aware. As I've grown this gift, I affirm that, just like Dad said that night, I am safe to encounter this wild, wonderful world.

This very moment—a-blink-of-an-eye, a mere *nth* in the expansive Now—is a good time for you to be alive, aware, and write…right now.

6

Awareness

AFFIRMING A JOURNALER'S CONSCIOUSNESS

Use affirmations, one or all, adapting as desired.

I wake to my life's full sensual experience and sharpen my awareness in my journaling practice.

I write my full panorama of sensations, emotions, thoughts, and intuitions.

I fully experience each precious moment instead of killing time by living unaware.

I encounter this whole, wild, wonderful world and write all about it.

I make space in my mind to allow inspiration to come to me now.

I zoom out and zoom in to be authentic in capturing both the big picture and the fine details as I journal.

I seek, stretch, morph, and mature to become fully alive
through the encouraging internal voice of my intuition
whenever I write.

I go outside and play to nurture awareness, accept
inspiration, and extend the reach of my imagination in
my Me Party journaling time.

Anywhere can be an infinite buffet for my physical,
emotional, mental, and intuitive senses. I consume
in the moment and then write the particulars.

I treat observation as a meditation of awareness as I
challenge myself to journal my whole truth.

I trust my intuition's response to the direction of my thoughts,
recognizing this guidance in real time and through my writing.

I stay present and open to the originality of the moment.

Write an affirmation about expanding awareness.

o Begin with either "I am…" or "I…" followed by an
  action verb in present tense, such as greet, dance, or
  tingle.
o Complete with heartfelt words to lift your spirit
  and motivate your growth.

6

Awareness

PROMPTING A JOURNALER'S PRACTICE

Choose a word or phrase,
and then journal what comes up.

o   Afraid of the dark

o   Biscuits

Complete a sentence and write more.

o   "I noticed an example of each of my
    senses—physical, emotional, mental, and
    intuitive—including…"

o   "When I was a child, I played make-believe by…"

o   "Now, I want to go outside and play, having a
    Me Party at…"

Create your own prompt and journal from it.

o

7

Writing Perfection

Every word I write
is ideal in
intention and
expression for
the good of
my creativity.

THE STARS ALIGN

Veiled by the earth's shadow, the waning crescent moon hid amongst twinkling stars, lounging far from the drama in the speeding Pontiac as Dad drove Mom to the hospital moments before the stroke of midnight. While others on the streets were coming home from a Saturday evening out, Dad whisked her to my big entrance into our family's feature film as its newest character.

For fifteen years since that night, I had imagined my birth like a Hollywood movie…

My mother, dressed in pastel satin, squeals as she discreetly pushes three times to build suspense, then my newborn cry rouses everyone in the delivery room to gasp and gaily giggle. After nurses bathe me, they delicately press powder onto my porcelain complexion to cover the newborn shine, then the doctor holds me high for the overhead shot and audience inspection.

Ah…breathtaking.

I tilt my head just so, blow a bubble, and blink my sparkling blue eyes. The camera lingers, remaining tight on me as I am presented to Mother, who receives me like a coveted Oscar, her mascara holding firm through a smattering of joyful tears as she instantly forgets the agony of delivery to scrunch her face at my astounding cuteness. She bites her lip softly, pondering her leapfrog over Elizabeth Taylor on the A-List, then positions me perfectly to her breast—not to feed, just to cuddle—as the camera nuzzles in for the close-up of her gleaming white smile and my angelic face. I coo, and for the first time in this life, I get the last word. Fade out…

Fade in on harshly contrasting reality. Now, I am almost driving age but have that same goo-goo face after sharing my vision of that storied night. Momma laughed as we cut summer squash at our country kitchen's round oak table, preparing them for parboiling and freezing.

"Nope, honey, it didn't happen like that," she said, brushing the slices into a big bowl before grabbing another squash from the 5-gallon bucket and placing it on the cutting board. "Once we got to Georgia Baptist, you began to come out while I was peeing."

Afraid I would cut myself, I set the knife aside as I realized the bitter truth of my birth: I crowned while she evacuated her bladder! I know we were both anxious to get the whole thing over, but geez. I steadied my hand and cautiously picked up the knife, making a cut and noticing a worm hole. Without looking for the larva, I tossed the whole thing in the compost bucket and grabbed another squash before asking incredulously, "What if I had drowned?"

She didn't skip a beat. "Oh, you were still attached to me."

I put the knife down again as I gave her a quizzical look.

"The cord? Not cut yet?!" She gave the squash a wild hit with her knife. "Besides, the hospital had a basket in the toilet just in case."

I glanced at my knife and then rested my hands in my lap. Maybe she was joking; she seemed to think it was funny. I took her seriously; I thought it was disgusting. The awe-inspiring miracle of birth? Eww, gross.

"Yep, it was over quick. No sooner was I on the table than the doctor said, 'Congratulations, Mrs. Smith, you have a perfect little boy!'" She stopped and flashed her loving, gap-toothed smile. "And you are, baby." Using her knife, she pointed at the squash in front of me. "Now, keep cuttin'. There're more buckets of squash in the utility room, and Papa's out picking more in the garden."

Working to keep the slices uniform, not too big and not too small, I pondered how, upon my initial wailing expression, some random obstetrician uttered the first words I ever heard on planet Earth, positively planting perfection in the fertile soil of my pure mind for all other thoughts to try and grow around.

I tried to ignore her 'being birthed into a commode strainer' story with a theatrical roll of my eyes, then continued the chore while I shifted my thoughts to what I wanted to be when I grew up. Like most kids, my dreams had already changed a thousand times, but the current answer was clear and simple: I wanted to be Robert Redford. I wanted to be the picture-perfect blond Hollywood actor with a million-dollar smile who could convincingly play the outlaw with heart like he did in *Butch Cassidy and the Sundance Kid*, the charismatic con artist who stole for good in *The Sting*, and the motivated yet conflicted writer in *The Way We Were*. He was convincing in jeans jumping off a horse onto the dusty plain as well as in a tux getting out of a limo onto the red carpet. With a role as a famous journalist in *All The President's Men* on the horizon, my future fantasy cemented. I wanted to be just like him, an unaffected star at home with my vast range of perfect possibilities.

Weeks later as my farfetched fantasy faded, I was back in high school as a snotty yet sensitive junior, looking for inspiration everywhere as this was decision time on what I would do for the rest of my life. I was thrilled when my best friend Sharon showed me her new astrology paperback. I knew it might give me more insight into the roots of my being, but I had to be quiet about it since, in my rural school, many minds were small. This investigation had to be hush-hush because, to some, the zodiac was "of the devil."

"I am *such* a Virgo!" I whisper-screamed to Sharon in the empty classroom before the bell.

She looked over my shoulder at the book, her cheeks rosy with excitement. "I thought so when I read it. You *are* detail oriented—"

"And highly organized and afraid of blood," I said, preening.

"Always neat and hate messes," she enthusiastically concurred. "And hypercritical!"

I jerked my head back as if she'd taken a swing at me.

"I didn't mean that as a cut," she said. "But it's true. You do analyze everything to shreds—ah, I mean, you, ahhh… see each situation from all sides?"

Sharon had dug her hole, and even though she was right, I exercised my critical nature to let her lie in it. Haughtily, I put my nose back in the book. I mean, really, I knew I was analytical because I'd lived with myself for sixteen years. She just didn't need to be so eager to gush about it. I wondered what *her* horoscope said, but before I could flip to Aries, a sentence jumped off the page: "Virgo loves perfection."

At that time, I thought incessantly analyzing things was an incredibly good trait and felt a boastful pride in it. Living my vision as a perfect Virgo, I recognized how perfection was prized in math, punctuation, and a clean typing test. Of course, I was too immature to realize I could choose what to believe about myself, even while doing so repeatedly as teens often do, changing personality traits like clothes. Instead, the pervasive plant of perfection was generously fertilized in my consciousness by the astrology book's statement and the judgment of others. This led to achievements like graduating with honors and a beautifully organized closet, but it wreaked havoc by nearly choking out most blossoms of creativity. The battle between the in-the-moment inspiration and the lifelong quest for perfection was akin to the deadly conflict pitting Butch and Sundance against the U.S. Marshals.

The bell rang, and students began to unwillingly wander into the classroom. Most didn't like English, but I had done well under the tutelage of other teachers. However, while in classes with Mr. Driskill, something shifted. He cheerfully encouraged my best work. For the first time when writing essays, I felt I could be my usual studious self while also creatively playing with subject matter.

My self-assured attitude thrived, and soon, I was able to invite humor into my writing. When given open-topic essay assignments in his class, I wouldn't start until I had a topic that not only fit my interests but also allowed me to enjoy the process. For example, we had to write a definition essay. Being a somewhat-shy smart aleck, I could not stop giggling as I pondered the topic "What is a Toilet?" Immaturity prevailed with the content while my skills steered structure, grammar, and word choice to ideal effect with comic spirit spot on. Though nervous when I turned it in, I received high marks. I guess it's fortunate I had buried my humiliation from the previous summer of discovering that a toilet could be a place for live birth. Mine. I knew I would never ever write about that.

When the angst of meltdown around Dad and the Tempest convertible fiasco led to a poem, I mustered the courage to show it to Mr. Driskill. To my delighted surprise, he said, "This is great," and then to my abject horror, he added, "Let's publish it in the school newspaper." Fearful thoughts flew through my mind as my trust in him took over and pushed an "okay" from my mouth. My best defense of outing my emotional turmoil to the entire school was knowing I had two other articles in the next edition. I also remembered the moans and groans in English class whenever poetry was brought up, realizing who in the student body reads verse anyway? So, out it came, and for a couple of days I held my breath, ready to defend or flee if challenged, yet only one person mentioned it: Sharon. And she liked it, describing all the reasons why. I felt a little more confident, and life moved on.

And before Christmas break, Mr. Driskill told me I would be the next editor of the yearbook. When I said, "But I don't know what to do," he replied, "Sure you do. What you don't know, you'll learn. You'll be great!" And that was that, and I was.

From Mr. Driskill, there were no doubts. To him, goodness and perfection were very different. Thus, I was able to experiment with creativity and express with words in a bigger way than ever. As I began to write, I felt more optimistic instead of holding my breath, waiting until I was finished to see if I pleased others...and sometimes myself. He gave me a gift of feeling safe in the act of writing, and as I relaxed, the words flowed like never before. As self-trust built, I found that if I felt good while writing, I generally liked the result, and for the most part, others did too. I kept the focus on my integrity and joy in my process.

Though a tad more mature in college, I was challenged with the responsibilities of living away from home and the faster pace in classes. One frustration came in a beginning acting class when I had to write a daily journal to help with backstory for performance. A requirement spanning the entire quarter, I thought writing a journal was an absurd waste of time, but of course, with a grade at stake, I did it anyway. Though I passed the assignment and the class, I'm not sure the journal enhanced my stage abilities as I wrote about how people behaved as they waited for a bus and such. Oddly enough, decades later, I still remember journaling about how the fresh fall leaves left imprints on the sidewalk after a rain. I was mesmerized by the enchanting image and how students walked over them without noticing. I got into the assignment and considered what emotions were behind others' actions, even inadvertently looking at myself. I loved that the journal didn't have to be English 101 perfect, and the norms of editing were ignored. The words landed however they fell out, even if in messy lists. To fill the page quota, I scribbled drawings to illustrate the text, but I mostly blabbered about nothing, usually my feelings, most of which were negative. The "A" was nice, but the prized takeaway was a chink in the armor of perfection. I calmed my strictness of writing's duty to ink and paper.

So, after finding my personal voice and my growing spirit along the way, I loosened up my writing as I moved into my degree coursework in journalism. New skills found through writing for newspapers, magazines, and broadcast's radio, TV, and film enhanced my examination, approach, and process.

Five years after graduation, the idea of "personal journalism" incubated to include modified journalistic ethics as my practice unfolded in 1987. First was a commitment to journal the full truth just for me. Next, I exercised awareness, recognizing a lead as a prompt, questioning self and getting answers for expansion, uncovering personal facts in the form of thoughts, feelings, and actions, and doing all of this on the page. Then, instead of editing, I wrote other fresh discoveries and connections. And finally, I held safety, protecting the source—myself—and doing no harm, only good, using my words for compassionate personal growth.

In 2003, I was encouraged by my friend Jessie to formulate and teach a journaling class. In both the pages of my journal and in my head, perfection, the false-hearted fraud, blasted its message.

You've never written a curriculum for a class before. This is lunacy. Though you think you do, you don't know everything! You won't be able to answer all the students' questions!

The fact that I had 16 years of daily journaling experience and a college degree didn't matter. The messages multiplied, coming through in ground-shaking Surround Sound.

The students will wonder why you are teaching! They will ask for their money back. How embarrassing!

I wobbled, dizzy from being berated.

Who do you think you are?

And there it was: Never Mind throttled me with the most perfect attack on one's self-esteem.

I felt even more stupid when I admitted this to Jessie.

"No one knows it all," she calmly said, soothing my fears. "You learn by doing, and that's true for teaching."

Her statement made sense, and the warm energy behind it felt familiar, like that I had received from Mr. Driskill as he dismissed my doubts with challenges to grow while supporting me with straightforward encouragement. Plus, her statement was true of my practice of personal journalism, so I wrote how my solid commitment to this practice provided an ongoing opportunity to write about and examine my life, including my fears. I used perceptions from all my senses, notably emotions and knowledge, to engage my intuition and bolster my beliefs. I believed my thoughts, feelings, and choices, as well as both my spoken and written words, manifested my world, so I took this as a springboard to affirm this truth for myself.

> My journaling practice supports me to be open, aware, and creative in growing and sharing good.

I recognized that my worries were in my head, while my heart already had the good feeling. That trust, however small, was mighty enough to help me let go of needing all the details before I began. So, what if I tripped and fell? It certainly wouldn't be the first time. In doing so now, I would learn something new about both falling and getting back on my feet. The fringe benefit of this process was how my actions and energy fueled the completion of the class curriculum.

Shedding shame, I gained confidence through humility to admit to myself that I didn't know everything. Squirming and sweating in the first class, I felt guided to tell the truth.

I began the habit of starting each class with an affirmative admission, saying, "I am here to teach and to learn. I don't know it all, but hopefully you'll learn something from me as I'm sure I'll learn something from you. And when you ask something I don't know, we'll discover it together and both learn." I felt an odd, comforting power in my vulnerability, and wow, what a relief!

In that first class, I introduced the concept of affirmations to oppose Never Mind. Whatever issues the students shared, I surprised myself as I extemporaneously spoke an affirmation created just for them. They feverishly wrote theirs down and even wrote those crafted for others. I had no idea that once I got out of my own way of being concerned about the perfect word, the perfect punctuation, and the perfect pronunciation in my scripted curriculum, the flow from knowledge, feeling, and intuition would deliver ideal connection and harmony. It felt otherworldly yet quite natural. I smiled a new smile that night. And after class, I further saw how my personal journalism practice brought together all the gifts I had gathered throughout studying, sharing, speaking, and living. Plus, my own practice deepened.

A year or so later in an advanced journaling class, I sat at a table talking about Never Mind with four women of various ages and backgrounds. Someone brought up astrology, so it folded into our discussion. No matter their signs or status, they all had the perfection bug, yet their gifts twinkled like stars to me.

Yvonne laughed. "My Never Mind tells me I shouldn't write anything I wouldn't want to read."

"Wow," I said. "It's like the cliché 'if you can't do it right, then don't do it at all.'"

"Exactly! I figure since I'm the Gemini twins, I've got two heads and perfect reflection. So, I am formulating the entire story in one of my heads and pre-reading it in the other before I take the chance to write it."

"Even with a journal entry?"

A dopey smirk formed, her eyes widened, and then she slowly nodded her head up and down. Everyone cracked up.

"There's no way of knowing until you write it," I said. "And isn't that a lot of pressure on yourself while you try to journal? Besides as we journal without review, we get insight and emotion back organically as the practice works its magic. There's no freedom for those of us being staunchly spied on by perfection. It's downright delusional. No offense."

Yvonne grinned and gave me a wink.

"So," I added, "you pre-judge your writing and never even get to the act."

Sounds like my dating life!" Yvonne said, high-fiving Vicky. As the laughter died down, she added, "Honestly, even glimpsing yesterday's words as I flip to a fresh page can stop me too."

Vicky interjected, "I am a Scorpio, and perfection stings my inspiration even more. I get this back-and-forth battle in my head when I try to write…" She bobbed her head from side to side, stating accusations in a husky drill-sergeant tone. "Stop this nonsense! You're making a fool of yourself!" Then she leaned her head forward and meekly encouraged like a fairy godmother. "Come on, Beautiful, you can do it! Write your thoughts!" Then she reverted to, "No, that's not right! Give up!" The sparks continued to fly between positive and negative charges. "Yes, Beloved Queen, that's right!" then "Wrong! Fail-yure!" then "Keep going, Sweetheart!" then "Puh-lease, you're lost in a fairy tale!"

As we howled at her performance, it was obvious to me that she'd been a tortured player in this scene through multiple takes while the lonely cursor, ready for action, blinked aimlessly on a sterile screen.

"This maddening dialogue inside your mind commands you to simultaneously start and stop like trying to drive with one foot pressing the accelerator while the other presses the brake," I said. "With keen awareness, listen to your internal dialogue with perfection, journal about it, and then make the decision on whether perfection resonates with your writing spirit or not. As you realize there is no balance as both desire and denial push and pull, reframe the dialogue by affirming a new truth. Replacing perfection may never happen, but recognizing it, knowing it, and building up the new belief you choose to live by will gradually turn down its volume."

"Some quiet so I could journal would be very nice," Vicky whispered.

"I guess I'm an Aquarius, but I know I'm an approbation addict," Olivia wholeheartedly admitted. "I'm always looking for not just any approval, but perfect, official approval for my journaling."

As she stared at me, no doubt awaiting my agreement, I asked her if that makes it hard to complete her writing.

With more than a hint of sarcasm, she roared, "What do you think?! I judge the judge, so imagine how constantly I judge myself. Like always! It's a very wicked game."

Everyone's eyes were on Olivia, holding back laughter as they awaited her response.

Olivia sighed, adding, "And that's why journaling is very difficult because there's no one to give consent but me! And who am I?!"

"Tell me about it," Isobel said. "Libra or not, there's no balance. Perfectionism *is* my Never Mind, my dominant fiend."

This wise businessperson knew her issue was an inside job.

"In sixth grade, I began the lengthy battle with extreme self-consciousness and doubt while I excelled at school, and then at work, even in leadership roles. My writing was always celebrated, but these compliments just slid off me like I was made of Teflon."

I could feel how complacent she had become with the convenience of these reasons to avoid facing her journaling. She donned them like an exquisitely tailored power suit.

"So, like Olivia, you can't find the perfect authority to give you credit. However, mere mortals simply aren't good enough for you," I said. "That's like knowing you must reach for the stars, but there's no spaceship. You are never ever worthy... yet trying but going nowhere."

I instructed them to write these beliefs along with me, so we could examine and rewrite them together. I knew our internal mantras were perfect for the way we were, but now we could create something new, something affirming positive growth.

In the silence as we wrote, I could feel the mood shift as we opened to new possibilities of encouraging awareness and positive self-evaluation instead of the negative one of unattainable perfection. And it struck me that many of us read our horoscope just for fun. Sometimes, it feels spot on but doesn't turn out that way. Other times, it seems silly, if not ridiculous, but comes true. Still others, it doesn't make sense and shows no relevance in our lives whatsoever. So, if there's a jovial, curious attitude when approaching astrology, why can't we look at perfection that way? Honestly, either might be a dream come true, a personal passing fancy, or just a laugh. Or they shine light on a goal, and we feel that excited energy percolating inside while also knowing that, as we explore, there's no telling what might be stirred up and situated in our path as we create. And I know for me, that not only feels sensational, but it also feels real.

As a writer reflecting on life in your journal, consider the ways you move beyond the limited thinking of fear, worry, and doubt. By exploring them in writing and affirming their opposite, they are ideal in how they show you what needs to be shifted and cultivated for positive enhancement. Remember that to do something well, you must first give yourself permission to learn, and that often includes mistakes and changes. Releasing perfection frees the process to start while opening you to new experiences and growth. Doing your best is the goal, not making it perfect. In essence, if you do your best, could you really do anything more? So, in every moment, your best *is* as perfect as it gets.

On the other hand, perfection often implies when reaching a pinnacle and arriving at the very top, this is it! The view is unlike anything you've ever seen...but you're stuck! Unless your imagination can create wings or a ladder to a cloud above, and that cloud has some solidity, there's nothing else to grow and nowhere else to go. However, even with this bright spot of personal recognition on the continuum of your evolvement, you aren't at the end point. You can't be because, like you, creativity is constantly growing, so there's always more to learn. Your choices create your world, so as you are aware of seeming ups and downs, you enlarge your consciousness and broaden your spirit. With that, you add a vital piece to your collective good. Eventually, like it or not, you have to start your descent back down, and then you realize—Wow!—this is both a new view and a new experience. And off you go!

Since perfection is the ultimate in self-judgment, redefine perfection to fit your spirit. To me, perfection is the ability to create in the moment, allowing inspiration's spark to light up imagination's playground throughout my journaling practice, knowing that process is ideal with each breath just as life is. All is well and still growing.

Also, as you journal and consider the essence of your practice—right now, not reviewing the written words—empower the internal voice that notices something good. Temper your habit of noticing the "bad parts," or at least try not to make comparisons. Recognize the feelings of achievement and expression, and then take a moment to linger in them. Release doubt and worry that your journaling practice isn't producing the "right way." What matters is that you are journaling. Perhaps someday you'll realize that the steps and adjustments needed for growth are inherently instilled within the practice itself. And you may notice this in retrospect upon recognizing you have shifted. For now, let it be, flow with your practice, and continue your special, developing brand of personal journalism.

Yvonne, the Gemini who tried to write the journal entry in her head before picking up her pen, discovered that putting a satin ribbon as a bookmark in her leather-bound journal produced two feats: first, it gave her an easy starting point for the next journaling session, one where she didn't have any fear of seeing and judging past entries. Additionally, when she closed her journal, the ribbon showed the bulk of pages she had accomplished as the marker moved ahead like constellations across a night sky. And Yvonne felt proficient without scrutinizing a single word.

Vicky, the Scorpio, found that sitting in her chair at her computer, lighting a candle, and meditating for fifteen minutes before putting fingers on home keys centered her. She encouraged her Never Mind to chatter and wear itself out far, far away from her royal throne. As the noise faded, she visualized her creative kingdom and invited the Queen to come forth to write. Over time, the meditation went from uninhibited disorder to fostered peace, a serene place to greet her true inner voice before safely and joyfully pouring it onto the page.

Olivia, the self-described approbation-addicted Aquarius, transformed by writing affirmations about herself as the authority while releasing judgment from the inside out. As she crafted each affirmation, it could take days to get it in the shape where it truly spoke to her spirit, and when it did, she took a metallic marker and drew a giant heart encompassing the phrase as both a sign of completion and a seal of approval.

And Isobel, the Libra who shielded herself from all good as if she was made of Teflon, found a way to let go of doubt through her affirmations. As she amassed these powerful statements within her computer journal, she soon followed her creativity to buy a special, sequin-covered journal just for them to be written in her own hand. As she pondered if the idea was too silly, she heard the noise Velcro made when unhooking the clasp. She realized that, unlike Teflon, this Velcro would always securely hold these personal gems of her spirit, easily open to uplift her at any time, and never ever let them slip away.

Some years after finding both humor and freedom in my journal, my consciousness changed the first time I saw a more mature Mr. Redford without makeup, far from airbrushed perfection. However, beyond the soulful expressions he created on the silver screen, his golden actions as a humanitarian and creative advocate jettisoned judgment. His smile, eyes, and spirit still dazzled. Redford's career was no longer my goal, but his light continues to inspire.

And though decades have passed, one life lesson lives on. Whenever doubt about journaling dims my spirit into the darkness of "I don't know what to do," I hear Mr. Driskill answer in my mind, "Sure you do. What you don't know, you'll learn. You'll be great!"

Much more than a memory, my teacher endures as a mighty mentor. Outside of my family guardians, Mr. Driskill was among my first trusted ones. He held a safe space for me to explore my creativity and sharpen my written expression, teaching me to trust myself and boldly do my best. His confidence was key in forming the foundation for my spirited creative self, serving me as both writer and teacher. For his stellar guidance still lighting my way, as well as opening my eyes and heart to others like Jessie who recognize and encourage the good in me, I remain grateful.

Just as movies are larger-than-life projections of make-believe on a screen, perfection is a grand illusion. Keep journaling and move ahead with your writing and your growth. Remember that perfection is not the end point; personal expression is the everyday goal. Creativity is the only thing that's perfect, yet it constantly expands, and how it was the moment before is equally perfect to how it is now and how it will be next. So, pick up your pen or place your fingers on the home keys and journal because you are a writer doing your best.

Stars align all the time. According to how we believe, they arrange ideally as we write. Maybe you see that as a miracle; to me, it's simply a good use of creativity. Even with any dramatic pushing, sweating, and screaming of birthing an entry in your journal, keep writing and grow in your practice. Spark inspiration, spotlight imagination, and deliver your expression at the right time. Free of the limiting vision of perfection, the vast range of possibilities is bright. You'll see the illumination as your journaled words shine their unique light and a star is born.

7

Perfection

AFFIRMING A JOURNALER'S CONSCIOUSNESS

Use affirmations, one or all, adapting as desired.

When perfection attempts to intimidate or silence me, I write its messages, affirm their opposite, and keep journaling.

I am always growing up. My writing lifts me to be my best.

Imperfections offer guidance to growth in writing and in life.

Now, my writing is "right." Adjustments for betterment are inherently instilled within my practice. I continue evolving.

Liberated from perfection, I employ goodness in my goal to focus on integrity and joy in journaling.

I find the words to express as I practice my personal journalism. My writing spirit soars.

As I journal, the only person I aim to please is me.

Without the perfection desired to make a grade or draw an audience, my journal is ideal for my purposes with my words landing on the page however they happen to fall out.

My thoughts, feelings, choices, and words are a springboard to affirm a better truth for myself on and off the page.

I applaud myself for my words, receiving this personal seal of approval while ready for more writing.

I celebrate and offer gratitude for my mentors, past and present. I affirm and remain aware for guidance.

Perfection is a grand illusion, so by simply doing my best in my journaling practice, my stars align.

Write an affirmation about transcending perfection.

- Begin with either "I am..." or "I..." followed by an action verb in present tense, such as laugh, transform, or surprise.
- Complete with heartfelt words to lift your spirit and motivate your growth.

7

Perfection

PROMPTING A JOURNALER'S PRACTICE

Choose a word or phrase,
and then journal what comes up.

- My birth

- A lesson from my mentor

- Zodiac

Complete a sentence and write more.

- "To me, 'perfect' is…"

- "My experience was both otherworldly and quite natural when…"

Create your own prompt and journal from it.

-

8

Writing
Commitment

I honor my spirit
through
focused intention
and
devoted action in
my journaling practice.

LIFE'S SENTENCES

"I do," the groom announced, his eyes bright.

Squirming on a hardwood pew while trapped inside a suit and tie, Momma's touch settled me down. I looked at my parents watching the proceedings, the sides of their bodies touching as they held hands, and this made me think that once those two little words were exchanged, there was no going back. This pledge was forever.

Then, the bride was asked the same tangled question by the preacher. Fully focused on the groom, she chirped, "I do."

While the preacher proclaimed, "commitment before God," along with terms like "countenance" and "asunder" that sounded like gobbledygook, this ceremony felt like Sunday morning church where words and ideas from the olden days were spoken. I guessed since everyone else seemed okay with it, I would be too. Besides, I didn't have a choice to be anywhere else.

With their union official, the preacher gave Frankie permission to kiss Charlie in front of everybody! And all lovey-dovey, the smooching commenced as the organist played and the crowd sighed.

At almost five years old, I had never been to a wedding, but I was sure ready for it to end. The pretty flowers and candles, the sparkly windows, and the fancy dress-up clothes could only keep me sitting still for so long.

The organ pipes roared, and I covered my ears as the beaming couple fled down the aisle, disappearing before we filed out. On our way to the reception hall, laughing teenage boys used shoe polish to paint words I couldn't read on the groom's lustrous car as teenage girls in their finery stood by, pointing and tittering.

Once inside, a loud gathering of people and a big spread of food met us, but my eyes were drawn to the tallest, frilliest, whitest cake I'd ever seen. For all the fuss Mom had made about the wedding dress, this confection was much prettier, plus I could smell it clear across the room.

"Let's get some food," Momma said, holding out her hand for mine as Daddy left to speak to some friends.

Pointing to the cake, I begged, "Please? Can I have a piece?!"

"Sweetie, you know you've got to wait for dessert until after you clean your plate," she said, guiding me toward the buffet. "And before cake, the preacher will say a few words."

I stopped on a dime, kicking at the linoleum, my lip puffed into a pout. "I don't want to hear the preacher again—"

Momma quickly bent down and took hold of my shoulders. "Now, that's not nice. You respect the preacher."

"Yes, ma'am."

Patting my arms and smoothing out my hair, she added, "Anyway, he's just gonna say a little prayer honoring the cutting of the bride and groom's first cake."

Suddenly sad, I asked, "They've never had cake?"

"Not as man and wife," she said, rising to usher me into the line.

Too little to be eye level with the food, I quietly shuffled in front of Momma down the long table. She exchanged pleasantries with those around us, mostly how she knew Frankie and his parents long before I was born. As she chatted with the lady behind her, I overheard the men across the table as they added cold cuts atop their jam-packed plates.

"Well, Frankie has an old ball and chain now," said the short one.

I listened more intently as I hadn't noticed the groom dragging anything as he walked down the aisle. Maybe I should have paid more attention. Anyway, he seemed happy, not like the shackled prisoners on TV shows.

Then the tall man said, "Glad it's him and not me. So, how's your ball and chain?"

As we cleared the buffet line, Momma handed me my plate, and I said thank you. Careful not to stain my Sunday clothes or drop anything on the floor, I looked over and wasn't surprised the short fella didn't have a ball and chain on his leg since I hadn't heard it rattling or clanking. I thought about asking him but remembered to have respect for my elders and not interrupt.

"She's fine," the short man replied, "in the ladies room nursing the baby, so I'm getting her some food before it's all gone."

"Yeah? All that's not for you?"

"Nah," he said, gobbling a cheese straw before nodding at the other guy's plate, asking with food in his mouth, "All that's for you?"

"Yessir. Free like me."

Suddenly, the gathered crowd began to cheer as the newlyweds reappeared. Hugging and glad-handing their way through the crowd, they headed toward the cake. Knowing I would have to gobble up every bite on my plate before getting a slice, I chewed as fast as I could.

The couple fed each other cake without a fork, shoving handfuls into each other's mouths, making a mess in what had to be their finest clothes. As people laughed, I wondered when Frankie's momma would come over and stop this foolishness. When someone finally cut cake for everyone, I got a piece and started eating it with my fingers as I walked behind Momma to a table. Even though the cake was moist and the icing was creamy, it just wasn't as good as the cakes she made. Still, it was cake, so I ate every crumb.

Back home, my change from suit to shorts was as fast as Bruce Wayne becoming Batman by sliding down the Batpole. I ran around the yard barefooted, playing with Princess. Her tail still wagging as we rested in the shade, I told her how the wedding was more fun than "regular" church because people laughed and there was cake.

Growing up, I understood my duty to go to church. Similarly, I had to go to school, and as much as I loved the freedom of barefoot summers, I was a good student and loved returning to the classroom. I never questioned my attendance or participation. My commitment, even without knowing the word, was solid. However, unlike public school, Sunday School didn't begin to match it. Though I tried with all my heart, my mind wasn't engaged. There were few enlightened "a-ha" moments and very little excited anticipation like how elementary school built on its lessons with what comes next. Sunday School couldn't engage me like reading, writing, and arithmetic, even penmanship and all the rest.

In church, services in the sanctuary were hard to follow and made little sense. Sitting in the hardwood pews was bad enough, but I had to endure it wearing church clothes. I started twitching before we left home, already constricted with my shirt tucked in my pants and a coat on top of that, plus there were the hard-soled shoes. Dad often struggled to button my top button and affix my clip-on tie. Confessing he also didn't like wearing ties was nice to hear but not enough, so to get me to stop wiggling, he promised to comb some of his Brylcreem into my hair. I didn't move a muscle as I liked the scent and enjoyed being like Daddy.

And like Momma, I loved music. Church music was nothing like her jitterbug hits or the Chubby Checker and Bossa Nova I sang and danced to as it played on my kid-sized record player. The screeching pipe organ reminded me of Nanny's melodramatic soap operas, but it was much louder as it echoed off the high ceilings. That instrument even made pretty Christmas carols sound like thunder. Now when someone played the piano, *that* was almost as lovely as when my Granny did. But even then, the words of the old-timey hymns tripped me up and, unlike my Disney sing-alongs, many church songs were not easy tunes to carry.

And I always loved hearing stories told to me with my classmates, but the sermon had all those ancient words I never heard at school or at home. The surroundings and circumstances weren't shared in a way I could understand, plus there were lots of characters, including multiple Marys, Josephs, and Johns. Though Jesus, like Batman, was almost always the star, there seemed to be new characters every week, and I couldn't keep up with who were good guys and who were bad guys. Though love was sometimes a part of the story, there was often a mistake that blazed up fury and judgment, leading to condemnation and eternal consequences.

Of course, I wasn't perfect either, and each time I got in trouble helped me to "know better." Alongside prayers at meals and bedtime, Mom and Dad taught me to say "please" and "thank you," to knock before I opened a door, and to treat people the way I wanted to be treated. The sweet ladies in

Sunday School emulated these manners and morals, but the sermons delivered lessons like how we are sinners and always will be, so we have to beg for mercy to ever be worthy of love. If Jesus loved me, as we proclaimed in Sunday School—even sung "...this I know"—what was the point of striving to be my best if I would always be judged as bad? Since I felt worthy of love from my parents and I was doing my best to be a good boy, the church's words left me feeling confused, fearful, even hopeless. I never ever felt good enough.

When I was 11, we moved from our suburban neighborhood to an intown rental while Dad built a house for us and another for Nanny and Papa side by side in the country. The rental was near my friend Hal's house and a few blocks from our church. Besides being on our own to jump on his trampoline, explore the creek, and visit neighboring friends to play games, we walked to church together.

One Sunday morning, seated in the new supersized sanctuary with its stark white walls, plush wine-colored carpeting, and crystal chandeliers, I noticed in the program that the sermon would be given by a visiting evangelist. I shrugged, fully expecting it to be the same ole, same ole. But when this minister spoke, his captivating delivery quickly caught my attention. With his words, the exotic Middle Eastern setting appeared in my mind like never before while the story brimmed with well-described people facing challenges and striving toward good. The lesson wasn't spoken as a demand but shared as a gift for my heart's decision, and I embraced it. And then, like every Sunday service, it ended with an invitation to join the church. Usually, this was my cue to coax some blood back into my legs for the walk home. On this Sunday when he made the offer, it seemed like just me in that 800-seat chapel. I didn't fret about the ribbing I might get from Hal and my friends. I didn't think of my parents. I simply felt moved. The evangelist's impassioned storytelling inspired me like never before.

I stood, and my feet's movement mirrored the rapid pace of my heart. Once I was way down front and the evangelist shook my hand, he turned me to face the congregation. Nervously, I stood with him, a young girl, and a new couple in town while the organ's closing song blared on. Then some of the congregants came up, welcoming me though I had been going there for most of my life. Next, I filled out a form as I answered a question from a church staffer on the whereabouts of my folks, sharing Mom was down the street cooking dinner and Dad was out working on our new house.

Anxious to go, I found Hal. He didn't tease me. He just asked if I wanted to come over to play after lunch, and I said sure. At home, I tore off my church clothes, neatly hung them up, and pulled on some shorts. Since Mom said it would be a little while before lunch, I went outside to the tiny backyard. Soon, she stuck her head out the screen door.

"The church just called."

"Was it the evangelist?!"

"What? No, it was our preacher."

I slumped.

She continued. "He said you are going to be baptized tonight. We'll need to get your clothes ready after lunch."

"But I'm going to Hal's!"

"Well, you can go after we're done."

As the screen door slammed shut, I turned back to the nasturtium seeds I had planted for my science project. When she hollered that lunch was on the table, I raced inside and washed my hands. Dad beamed, sharing his happiness that I was being baptized. I returned his smile. And then he mentioned they would be at church with me tonight, and I blushed, realizing this was a big deal. As we bowed our heads, I recited the "Give us, Lord, our daily bread" prayer and then covered my nervousness with Sunday dinner.

Even though I loved to swim, being dunked backwards in front of a crowd of people was terrifying. I didn't have my glasses on, and I was afraid that I wouldn't see the steps in the brightly lit, white marble baptismal. Our regular preacher did it quickly, making sure I did not fall, and then someone helped me out of the pool. Sopping wet, I was given my specs and guided to the changing room.

Back in church clothes, the freshly baptized were escorted through a side door, and I sat with my parents. I tried to listen, but my mind wandered from the preacher's routine rhetoric back to the story shared by the silver-tongued evangelist, no doubt already at another church, and how I was ready to get home to watch *The Wonderful World of Disney*.

Nothing much changed as I continued to go to church with Hal for the next few months. I asked questions of my Sunday School teachers about things I heard and didn't understand, but their responses evaded explanation, much less guidance, as each spoke of the mysterious with a twinkle in their eye. This reminded me of when I was a young child and asked adults the truth about Santa Claus. Those adults extended the enchantment of that belief that there was a magical man who delivered presents to every boy and girl in one night, and once I realized that he wasn't real, they seemed both relieved and saddened. Though I felt disgruntled at being tricked by them, I easily let it go as I found that I still loved the myth which, in a new way, upheld my love of the season. However, the church teachers' replies weren't answers to help me find the next step to open my heart, and this left me feeling disregarded, even wrong for asking.

Then when my family moved the twelve miles across the county, I missed my old friends who were going to a newly built school while I was going to a very old one by way of a very long bus ride. After gleefully attending three different schools, I was suddenly miserable. I couldn't relate to the kids. Despite the fact that the nearby town I moved from was very small, I was still labeled a "city boy," plus my education there was better, so I was ahead in classwork and therefore harassed for being a "smarty pants," a "showoff," and a "brainiac."

Mom made plans and insisted I go with the new neighbor kids to their country church. Even though I wasn't enthused about the neighbors or church, her mandate silenced my voice. I felt guilty and thus obligated. This little white church nestled under trees where members parked here and there on the packed earth. Thankfully, there was no organ, just a piano, in the unadorned chapel. The congregation numbered less than half the kids in my eighth-grade homeroom. While able to blend into the hundreds at the church in town, here I felt all eyes on me in a worse way than I did at my new school. Though everyone was nice enough, the service overflowed with shame and repentance from the loud calls of the Bible-waving preacher to the yelled responses of those in the pews. I felt alone and threatened in close quarters. I didn't belong.

With my arms crossed and heels dug in, Mom demanded I try again. I shouted that I could study my Bible at home, something I had never done before. Though I knew she was at a loss for ways to get me involved in this backwoods area, plus we both struggled with my grandparents living with us while their house next door was being finished, I proved to be the most steadfast in stubbornness. So, after my weeks of not backing down, Mom moved on.

Months later as I began to make friends at school and the name-calling subsided, the guilty obligation of church remained active in me. I cautiously visited my new friend Sharon's rural church, which was lovely with a nice-sized congregation, including some kids I knew from school. Though less primitive and without shouted replies, the fire and brimstone directive didn't spark inspiration. My rebellion solidified, and

I let Mom know it was my decision whether to go to church or not. And just like that, leftover confusion and loss about religion were all my own.

Even though I didn't study the Bible at home, I enjoyed fellowship with my new friends, and I communed with nature by taking long walks in the old growth forest across our rural road and floating in the backyard pool at night under a dazzling array of stars. I listened to music, made good grades, and held leadership roles at my school. I read and wrote outside of homework, encouraging me to think, understand, grow, and feel better about myself. But as I continued to engage in nightly prayer, I still believed God was outside of me as I was taught. And though I felt I had to obey Him, I didn't know Him, much less understand how He could be in Heaven and in my heart too.

When I left home for university a hundred miles away, the distance and being around other teens with varied life experiences brought recognition and release of some negative messages I had acquired. Like the little boy ditching Sunday clothes for shorts, I dropped the dogma I was taught that other religions were "wrong" and therefore "sinful," and I carefully explored, finding some other faiths interesting, accessible, and a little enlightening. Like discovering that I felt good dressed in preppy clothes, my developing awareness allowed me to see how a variety of people felt happy and harmonious living their chosen beliefs. I assumed one would fit me best and be a truth I could embody in my future. I really wanted that.

Just after Dad's gift of the floor lamp and my purchase of a personal computer—both revolutionizing my journaling—a coworker gave me a copy of *Emmanuel's Book: A Book for Living Comfortably in the Cosmos* by Pat Rodegast and Judith Stanton. She had noticed I was drawn to her copy and felt I might like my own. And I did. Though I remained skeptical of religion, and at the time "spiritual" meant the same thing, I didn't see this book as either. Even though there were chapters about Christ, there were others about behavior and feelings, as well as evolution and something called karma. Mostly, the book posed simple questions and furnished brief answers. Some read like poetry and others were adorned with intriguing, childlike sketches. Exploring "inner spirit and outer world" felt a little too wacky, but the guidance seemed grounded for my everyday life. Like the Bible, it still presented ideas I could not wrap my head around, but whether it was the relatable language or the place I was in, I spent time reading, pondering, and journaling about them. And for those I didn't understand, I didn't feel pressured since I was feeling what I felt from the visiting evangelist in church when I was 11. The soulful magnetism of the words inspired me, and I felt enriched. I discovered other books, received referrals, and kept exploring.

Soon, I worked up the nerve to visit a recommended church. The auditorium had no religious symbolism on display, so I quickly took a seat. Though the New Thought service featured a talk, some singing, and a collection plate, the teachings were universal and affirmative, pulled from many traditions, as well as philosophers, metaphysicians, scientists, authors, and artists. Over the weeks, I especially enjoyed the variety of music shared, but there was no organ—Woo-hoo!—as various performers were accompanied by piano, guitar, or harp. Though some songs were original, current hits and standards also aligned with the week's topic. As a music lover, realizing the all-inclusive spirituality of certain everyday songs was exhilarating, leading me to hear all genres of tunes differently through my broadening perspective.

However, even though the message was accessible and inspiring, I was taken aback by the reverend's humor, as well as the attendees' laughter and applause. Before I knew the meaning of intuition, it guided me to the church's casual weeknight service, one without Sunday's bells and whistles. More importantly, it was led by a female pastor, something else new to me. With her warm, compassionate style, I felt comfortable while consciously engaged. I even began to feel part of a community who spoke a loving language I understood and yearned to live by. This eventually encouraged me to revisit the Sunday morning services. Soon, I enjoyed them, too, as I sang, applauded, laughed, and cried. I also jotted down words to prompt my journaling.

I realized I had never met words I could access around these concepts, words which illuminated truth to my mind, heart, and spirit. Words have always been my gateway to understanding and embracing a new subject, and with New Thought, no translation was necessary. And as I began to go beyond recognition to practice, my commitment sprouted. In my late twenties, I began to discover who I was spiritually, even though I still couldn't call it that.

By this time, I journaled daily on the computer, exploring life in my words. At first, I observed and recorded. Then I inquired, discovering how I once defined "discipline" as a reaction from others in authority to my being bad. Now, the term also meant my personal response to daily habits of being and doing good. Soon, I looked outside myself to investigate further, and then, unbeknownst to me, my questions became writing prompts. I would place a positive concept in my mind, such as how affirmations work, and I would scrutinize it in my words until I understood and accepted it, then I began integrating it into my life. This led to one of my first affirmations:

> I trust the process of using affirmations, and I embrace these positive statements with my mind and heart to grow my good.

On the flipside, I recall writing how I still bristled whenever Jesus was mentioned during a service. At some point, I became okay when shared in a verse, but if it was a Bible story, my anxiety and irritation flared. I journaled about my anger, and for years, I halted at the same dead end. Additional attempts flagged my fears, and over the years, my journaled words illuminated a path—and a lot of side roads—as I traipsed toward a truce.

I set aside the words and revisited memories of the paintings throughout the church where Jesus was kind, approachable, and wise, radiating love from most every wall. Still, as a little kid, I noticed Jesus usually gazed just to the side and up, never seeming to look at me. Ultimately, I realized that the church had no images of God, so my creative mind took what I had been taught to make one up. For the most part, the term "God" provoked a bearded, monolithic deity, but due to the feelings from Sunday School teachings and chapel sermons of judgment and punishment, I mostly visualized something like a cantankerous version of Santa Claus.

So firmly ensconced in my child's mind, God and Jesus were a juxtaposition of an old, harsh disciplinarian, worse than any mean teacher I ever had, alongside a sympathetic and caring young man. This made me question how the two were close kin. Honestly, I also remembered being confused about the interchangeability of "God" and "Jesus" when "Jesus was Lord," but so was "The Lord, Thy God." Jesus was also the "Son of God" while the Trinity was "Father, Son, and Holy Ghost." Holy Ghost? Since all this made my little head spin, I had long stopped thinking about it.

As an adult writing on this in my journal, I knew I had to deal with the word "God," especially since I was being faced with the term anew in both readings and at services. "God" was prevalent in New Thought—just rarely "Lord," Trinity," and such as far as I could tell—and I was okay until my grown-up head spun when Sunday's new minister said,

"God isn't up there on High, but everywhere, in every being, and in everything. Oh, and by the way, God is genderless."

With my mind dizzy again, I clung to the simple phrase accepted from the childhood meal prayer that "God is Good." Slowly, I began to accept God was not a guy in the sky, much less a white guy, then not even a guy. Lightning did not strike me down, so I tried on the idea that God is an energy, infinite and ever-expanding. This concept slowly began to make sense and then started to bring comfort. Still, words are my thing, and "God" was a powerful term with a lot of baggage. I needed to put it aside for a synonym, so I surveyed and sorted through the options.

I felt at ease in the lore, music, and symbols of Native American culture, and I found peace with the term "Creative Spirit." My heart warmed. The words felt natural to my tongue and ear. And down the line, I abbreviated it to "Spirit." And then, with belief that there is no separation between Spirit and myself, I began to use spirit with a lowercase "s." Still respectful and very much the same unfathomable energy, the little "s" helped bring spirit into both universal and individual truth. My nature, my passion, my character: all spirit. Big "s" or little "s" doesn't matter. There is no division as spirit is spirit. Monumental, magnificent, and all encompassing, this oneness included me too.

Eventually, I found similar meaning with the word "creativity." I felt possibility, wholeness, and renewal. Creativity is constant, enlivening my gift of choice as to what I think, feel, and believe. And through my personal truth of being created of creativity to be creative, all human spirits are part and parcel, a portion of, yet still integral to, the whole. Spirit is everywhere, in me and every human, animal, plant, and microbe, in the Earth, in the sky, and far beyond the stratosphere, also in the water I drink and the air I breathe. In my every thought and every journaled word. In all creation. So, all is one.

I then endeavored to live my beliefs for the best of all beings every moment. Since journaling was already a commitment to expression, once I consciously added self-growth, the two became indivisible. Both are deeply personal decisions. Once on this path, I exercised awareness through journaling of my thoughts, feelings, observations, words, and deeds. I grew this commitment as I exercised my journaling passion, and I found my path to greater happiness and harmony. My practice became a private service every morning, my personal relationship of spirit in creativity. My journaling grew along with me.

I became aware of creativity everywhere. As I continued to read inspirational books, explore spiritual and secular music, hear varied viewpoints and traditions, and attend services and gatherings, I grew respect for the paths of others while finding words, stories, and rituals that brought a new light to my own. This supported healing for my Christian upbringing as I recognized and honored its place in my personal development. And as I learned more about the historical times when Jesus lived, my mind and heart opened, illuminating the universal truth in Jesus's teachings.

Around this time, I recalled and journaled about my claiming victory over Mom after our move to the country. With each word journaled, my old wall began to crack. Like those tight neckties and hard-soled shoes, church as it was in both town and country didn't fit well. Standing up for myself was important in my growth, and I gave thanks, but I also recognized how my firm stance had held me stuck for years. So, I journaled more to forgive Mom. As the person I talked with the most through any mood or situation, Mom strengthened my voice and expression, allowing me to safely show my emotions and often mirroring them back to me. I recognized that for each argument, there was an abundance of happy times too. This truth of the love we shared filled me with gratitude and sparked the strength to journal to forgive myself. And though some rubble remains, that stubborn wall of mine crumbled, letting in light to open a newfound level of vulnerability and spirit.

I reclaimed a foundational truth I learned as a child, one which shows up similarly in religious traditions: "Do unto others as you would have them do unto you." My parents not only taught me well and showed me compassionate examples day to day, they also trusted me to live this respect of self and others, both at home and out in the world. I believe that as long as I live a positive, creative life, contribute to the good of others, and aspire to do no harm while making amends when I do, I am living well. I believe my life is created from my thoughts. These thoughts become my beliefs, and through the opportunities I attract and the choices I make, they become my reality. So, if I use my thoughts to be hurtful or hateful to others, or see myself as privileged, better than others because of my race, gender, nationality, or any other factor, including my beliefs, I add to the violence in both my inner spirit and outer world. But if I cultivate a commitment to use my thoughts toward creativity, growth, and love, I contribute to the compassion and freedom in the world from the inside out, starting with myself. Every day, this unification is supported by my journal writing.

In childhood when others asked me, "What religion are you?" I felt defensive at their attempt to put me in a box. Though the town we lived in had just over ten thousand residents with an assortment of Christian denominations and a single Catholic Church, I learned of the reasons other faith paths were wrong according to the person who was judging it. At a young age, I knew that by sharing what church I attended brought on judgment. I recall making a friend in my neighborhood whose family went to a different Christian Church than mine, and once I heard opinions on that denomination from both adults and peers, it made me question how my buddy believed. With this difference, I never accepted his invitations for visits. And years on, I carried this into a world where I met Catholics, Jews, Jehovah's Witnesses, Hindus, Muslims, Buddhists, and folks who worshipped Mother Earth, the sun, and the moon.

The world seemed to have as many borders around religion than those of countries.

I observed there are numerous ways to segregate people through broad definition and lazy stereotype, so I journaled for clarity. I found life is not only simpler, but more beautiful, when I learn about others' lives and traditions through their words and actions. I felt if knowing any further definition is important to them, they would share it. So, these days when asked, "What religion are you?" I share that I live a creative life. I might elaborate that I feel spirited when writing each morning in my journal, sitting quietly, swimming laps, or walking in the woods, listening to all kinds of music, seeing an impressive performance, or drifting in the twinkling haziness before falling asleep. It also includes doing my chosen work, as well as being with others in joy and in sorrow. I am inspired by all paths that lead to light.

Truthfully, I may stay closer to one path than others. And though loving and uplifting, there is no tradition or speaker on Earth that can provide the last word for me. I believe in a life where I choose what lifts me and lights my way the best with each breath. And why not? All I really have in life is the Now, and this moment is ever changing as creativity is timeless, ever present, and always expanding...and I am a part of that. And really, there is no "last word" as each leads to the next word and the next. As such, I am committed to creative growth.

And I do my best to respect others, wherever they are in their growth. I admire and benefit from the inclusivity that

12-Step programs offer each participant to discover "the god of your understanding." This can include a deity, another perspective such as a "Higher Power," or none at all, respecting everyone's viewpoint. And why not? In one way or another, aren't we all in recovery? Aren't we all striving to face and understand personal negativity and dependence in our efforts to be strong and vital one day at a time? I have heard it said that we are on this Earth to face challenges, make choices, and grow love as humans, so how can we do this without one another?

So, whether your perspective has angels and saints, or your belief in science has energy and quantifiable forces, that's wonderful! In case your heart is fueled by an intricate hero's journey, or your outlook jibes with the vibes of the everyday to live the "best life of your understanding," that's super! Or if your principles pulse and glow uniquely in your spirit, that's marvelous! For these and other viewpoints, I encourage you to profoundly feel, believe, and trust your commitment to support your journaling practice toward magnified meaning in pursuit of good, healthy living.

Just as your beliefs and path through life is up to you, your journaling practice is also a personal choice. You are the one who initiated it, so you are the only one who formulates the steps and rituals to grow commitment. This is harder to do, yes, but it's also a stronger commitment when personally created, nurtured, and maintained. You explore topics in the present, using the words of your understanding which bring clarity and inspiration, and your writing practice strengthens through living this creative life.

Commitment is freeing, never a burden. Commitment doesn't hold you through command and control; you hold commitment by questioning and building it as you honor and act upon it. Though commitment may seem forever binding, you always have a choice, and your choices create your life. Truly, commitment must be adaptable as you grow because if it's static or dogmatically aligned, it's stifling of creativity as boundaries are solidly fixed. Use your positive belief, growth-oriented attitude, and personal action to create your life's sentences which affirm and guide you now. And when it is time for an updated commitment, create anew. Growth means change, and as you experience your life's phases, you likely need to recreate your life's phrases. Count on your journaling and the support from your written words.

Following the beautiful example of abiding commitment shown to me daily by my parents, whose love spanned from "to have and to hold" all the way to "till death do us part," I embody a devoted focus to my journaling practice while also loving each moment and every interaction with inspiration and integrity.

Do I live and breathe writing spirit? I do.

8

Commitment

AFFIRMING A JOURNALER'S CONSCIOUSNESS

Use affirmations, one or all, adapting as desired.

I am a dedicated journal writer, always aware to collect topics and details while knowing an ideal place to safely write.

In journaling and life, commitment is freeing. Never a burden, commitment doesn't hold me; I hold my chosen commitment by honoring and acting upon it.

I count on the support from my written words.

Life-affirming commitment requires trusted belief, a positive attitude, and personal action.

Like all other beings, I am created of creativity to be creative. For myself, I journal.

I formulate the steps and rituals to honor commitment in my practice as I journal the words which define meaning in my life.

I always strive to know better, leaving behind blame, shame, and judgment while choosing light and love.

My journaling allows me to express every aspect of my spirit.

My commitments to expression and growth are indivisible. Both thrive in my writing.

I journal the words of my understanding, words I don't have to translate, words that instantly illuminate my truth.

When my intuition whispers, I listen and write.

My journaling practice sustains my soulful integration with the world, starting from the inside out through my committed use of words, heightening compassion and fostering unity.

Write an affirmation about solidifying commitment.

- ○ Begin with either "I am…" or "I…" followed by an action verb in present tense, such as immerse, gobble, or blend.
- ○ Complete with heartfelt words to lift your spirit and motivate your growth.

8

Commitment

PROMPTING A JOURNALER'S PRACTICE

Choose a word or phrase,
and then journal what comes up.

o   Seeds

o   A wedding and a reception

o   Shackled

Complete a sentence and write more.

o   "The lyrics to this song lift my spirit because…"

o   "I faced a challenge, made a new commitment, and grew when…"

Create your own prompt and journal from it.

o

9

Writing Procrastination

I treasure life
when I
designate and
take time
to write
in my journal.

RELEASE THE HOUNDS

The sun shone through the ice crystals frosting the skylights, and though the air was frigid outside, the tranquil atmosphere around the pool enveloped my near-naked body with tepid warmth.

That water's too cold. You'll freeze.

Dripping from my pre-swim shower, I gingerly tiptoed on the concrete decking to the edge of the placid pool, simultaneously trying to generate heat while not stirring up a breeze. No goose bumps, but I did raise another snarled warning.

Journaling won't heal you if you catch pneumonia. Go put on some clothes!

As I popped in earplugs and donned goggles, droplets of water flung from me onto the still surface, setting off precursors of waves to come, each concentric circle broadening then crossing one another before dissipating. I reminded myself of the truth that, winter or summer, this water is always 82 degrees. That's a higher temp than it is outside, plus as I swim, my body warms up from exercise.

Sitting on the edge, I carefully slid into the waist-deep water, and a shiver was met with gratitude for my commitment to good health. As I submersed my body preparing for my first lap, I gave thanks for having the pool all to myself. Though many, like me, were on holiday from work, they were probably watching football or preparing for parties. Others were getting ready for the end of the world.

The excited tone of New Year's Eve had a sharp edge this year. In my head, The Artist Formerly Known As Prince kept singing one of his old songs, now strangely relevant. Though lyrically bleak, it had a good beat and I could swim to it, so my strokes kept rhythm to his funky guitar riffs playing in my mind.

1999. Y2K. Just hours until the year, decade, and century changed. I pondered what would happen at midnight then managed to swim free of the fear in my head to consider resolutions. I was already exercising, eating right, doing a good job, participating in loving community, and journaling daily for over a decade. Hmm, I thought maybe I'll challenge myself to explore more in my journaling, then that idea was drowned out as the tune by Prince faded back up with its judgment and destruction.

Laps complete in my toasty oneness with the water, I inhaled before submerging. Blowing all the air from my lungs, I sank, positioned the pads of my feet on the pool wall, then pushed off. Staring at the bottom, I watched the smooth whiteness of the gunite go by. Like time moves on, the pool floor simply passed beneath me. I recognized how much I trust myself in the water, as if I'd made a pact with the surface to take me back in my moment of need. Unconcerned,

I focused on the water's volume and my heartbeat within it before spinning my body lengthwise to arise, face up, and float until my breathing calmed.

Back at the house, I took the lid off the pot of black-eyed peas that had soaked overnight, all bloated beneath a frothy layer of murk. Using the lid to secure them while leaving a small opening, I poured out the liquid, then rinsed and drained the peas again and again. This annual family tradition was for the New Year's Day meal. Though usually a happy time, as I looked out the window while the faucet filled the pot, a wave of worry passed through me again.

What if the predictions come true? What if the technology geeks' years of preparation doesn't solve the issues and the computers go haywire when the ninety-nine turns to zero-zero?

Actually in the computer's existence, nothing like this had ever been tested in real time. Placing the pot on the stove, I turned on the electric burner.

What if the grids collapse and there are massive power failures?

As the stove's eye began to glow orange, I dismissed the worry, then heard the cold, brisk wind hit the house as I began chopping onions.

What if the lack of air traffic control leads to midair collisions? What if the systems fail on the planes and they fall from the sky? Living only twenty miles from the world's busiest airport means certain death!

Chasing a squirrel, my dog woofed outside, yielding the minute I tapped my knuckle three times on the window.

Making eye contact with her, I said, "Good dog." As she proudly circled the backyard, I heard the neighbors' dogs pick up her note and yelp a chaotic choral response. No amount of tapping would stop them.

Neither would it hinder the hounds barking in my consciousness. As I stuck my head in the freezer to cool my burning eyes, I thought of how little I had journaled this morning and of how writing encourages my growth, my peace, and my spirit. I thought of how "what if?" is not only a great creative entry point as a writing prompt, but in the paws of Never Mind, it's used against me, stealing my creativity to bombard me with woe. Knowing a quiet mind is able to hear intuition over anxious thoughts, and also knowing that I can see both the good and the fear in my writing as it flows from me, I decided to take a half hour, even five measly minutes, to write something—anything—in my journal.

This is your last day on Earth! Party like Prince sang in his song! Besides, what if you lose computer files? All that writing over years and years will be for nothing! Why waste your final minutes on that? Journal tomorrow…if there is one.

I tossed the onions in the pot, then glanced at the happy-go-lucky birds on the feeder. They flew free while fear of a global nightmare haunted me in my own home. Obedient to the hounds, I set a timer and went upstairs for a long soak in a hot bath, decisively skipping out on journaling for the rest of the year.

Driving downtown in the late afternoon's fading light, I again rationalized that the way-too-early reservation for dinner was due to the traffic of the New Year's Eve holiday, but I knew it was really because of the qualms of what would happen when the clock struck twelve. No expense was spared on dining with friends as there was an outside chance all banking balances would soon be obliterated. My anxiety subsided as we laughed and ate appetizers, then my focus fixed upon the most sumptuous steak I had ever eaten. As I chewed, Never Mind chimed in.

Mmmm, just like the perfect last meal for a death row inmate whose life is ticking away.

I sighed, slowing to savor the flavor, finding solace in a taste of gratitude in the present. Swallowing, I jumped into our table's lively conversation, laughing to muzzle the doubts in my head.

Safe at home before eight o'clock, I flipped on the television, relieved to see Paris had moved into the new millennium just fine with the Eiffel Tower awash in colored lights as fireworks burst overhead. In Europe, they were still alive and celebrating.

At 11:59 p.m., I held my breath. Revelers on screen yelled, "Five, four, three, two, one, Happy New Year!" As "2000" flashed on the screen, I sat quietly, awaiting annihilation…and then suddenly, I fully exhaled, acknowledging that the TV was still on, showing the partyers in Times Square celebrating the release of the old and the beginning of new possibility, all sealed with a kiss as confetti rained down. Maybe North America would follow Europe and be okay. I turned off the tube and took my fading fear to bed.

When I woke the next day, the sun was out, the coffee brewed, the birds flitted around the feeder, and the TV buzzed to life by pushing one button on the remote. All was well, and I was safe. Still, I ignored my journal. While downing coffee and crunching granola in my stress hangover, the news anchor told a story about Atlanta's first baby born in the new year, just seconds after midnight, then added a note of an anxious hospital staff ready with generators in case of power failure. She added, "Mother and baby are both doing well."

The peas and collard greens were cooked, and my college football team's bowl game wasn't on for hours. Like everywhere else, the pool was closed. Recognizing yesterday's leftover fears alongside the serenity of this day's gift, I pondered what I would do with my time.

With my last cup of coffee in hand, I climbed the stairs to the office and booted up the computer, noticing all the files in place. I opened my journal document and saw the scant few words I'd written the morning before, noticing my doom-and-gloom attitude regarding the extravagant dinner: "It better be good." So, I began journaling with that thought, a quick sentence about the nice time had with friends and then affirming the truth that writing, like swimming, was always good, no matter the form or the outcome. Journaling always served a worthy purpose and would until the very end.

Pausing to scratch my head, I realized that even with the anticipatory weight attached to January 1 and the beginning of resolutions, the day seemed just like every other day. Despite my nervousness from the day before, only the date had changed. I took a deep, cleansing breath. Like the calendar which moves forward without concern, I, too, could move ahead without making a conscious decision to do so. So, why not be conscious and intentional of my choices? And why was I procrastinating in doing what I really loved to do? I have had lots of experience with procrastination, and I know it is Never Mind's mongrel let loose to growl its deceits and denials to keep me in the same place by chasing my own tail.

As I stared at the blinking cursor inviting my entry, it happened just like any other day of any other year. I felt a jerk in my stomach.

Ooh, I could use a snack!

And I obeyed. As I rushed down the stairs to the kitchen, I remembered I had recently eaten, then realized that the jumpy movement I felt in my stomach probably had little or nothing to do with hunger. Still, since I was there, I explored options in the pantry rather than exploring expression in writing. Procrastination wagged its tail as I tossed a bag of popcorn in the microwave. The kernels popped like firecrackers, making me even more jittery. Why was I nervous? I had survived the end of the world! And why did the blankness of a page spook me?

Sitting at the desk, I stuffed my mouth with handfuls of popcorn. Crunching away on faux fuel for writing, I noticed my fingers had a sheen.

Don't want that sticky mess clogging the keyboard.

After taking the bowl to the kitchen, putting it in the dishwasher, then washing my hands, I sat down at the computer and licked my lips.

Chapped! Where's the lip balm?

So, I headed to the bathroom to grab that, then back in my office chair with fingers in place where I typed half a sentence before receiving a message from my bladder. As if I were a dog on a walk, procrastination urged me to pee on every post. Hands off home keys and off again to...

With that out of the way, I glanced at the clutter on my desk.

Straighten up. It's the only way to really make space for new writing.

Even though I would just be journaling on the computer, my awareness was caged. Then my phone rang. It was Mom, who I just phoned yesterday.

Gotta talk to her! It is *a holiday!*

As she shared about being too tired to stay up to watch worldwide mayhem, I glanced at the clock on the computer and noticed a new email, so I scanned it while chatting. We traded I love you's, and then I snapped the phone shut. As I bit off a fingernail while wondering what else I needed to do, my energy sagged.

Often you listen to the inner voice that's the loudest, and procrastination yaps like an over-caffeinated Chihuahua, wearing you down until you give in to its whining by petting, cuddling, and baby-talking to its every need just to shut it up. But to journal with best intention, you have to pull focus away from Never Mind.

Decide what you want: either choose to use your energy to procrastinate or channel it to persevere. You can create excuses, excuses, and more excuses, or you can act on the goal of your heart's commitment. You will use your creativity one way or another. You can waste it on worry, or you can use it to engage with writing and progress in your passion.

To clear the path for journaling, plan ahead. Contemplate your state of needing to eat, drink, or pee, and take appropriate action. Have lip balm handy at your desk. Turn off the phone and shut down email, knowing you can check later, acknowledging how multi-tasking divides attention on all things trying to be accomplished. Then choose to sit and write without interruption from outside or inside yourself. Maintain full focus and notice the cheerful anticipation of journaling. Trust that during this "me time," the chance is slim that the world will end without you, and if it does, finding out fifteen minutes later won't make much of a difference.

When I began my journaling practice, I had to fight against Never Mind's assumption that writing was "another thing to do." Some days were worse than others. I soon discovered my best time to write is first thing every morning, and I began to recognize that writing calmed me down while building concentration, focus, and motivation. Journaling is joy, it's in the moment, and it's creative. And it was important and good for me, so I fit writing into my daily life.

I started small. After graduating college and before purchasing a personal computer, every time I considered a commitment to journaling, procrastination howled.

This promise is monumental. Way too big! There's no time for this too.

It was near my birthday in 1984 when I came up with a silly sing-songy title for the exercise: "Remember That September." Now neatly labeled, the trial run had a time limit and a designated blank journal. On Saturday, September 1, I began meeting my commitment each night before bed, reminding myself that it was only for thirty days as I yawned and blinked and wrote. And it felt good to take the steps and fulfill this promise. Though I didn't continue with any regularity until my practice began in 1987, this experiment laid the groundwork and acknowledged how journaling could span my life by writing one day at a time. Interestingly, this action is the only birthday gift or celebration I recall from that year.

Like January 1, each day's slate is always clean. So, where do you start? The amount of possible writing prompts can be overwhelming. Truly, having none can feel the same. Getting started is just like making a resolution to lose weight or get married. Just as resolutions involve small steps each day like watching caloric intake or dating, journaling is a journey of one word at a time. Take the first step, starting where you are, and repeat.

Make a personal commitment and schedule writing time, even putting it on your calendar. On my paper calendar, I jotted in ink "JRL" every day, and it was usually the first thing I accomplished and circled. After a year or two of this, my commitment was solid, so I no longer needed to list and check it off. The practice had become as much a cherished part of my morning routine as a cup of coffee with cream. And this practice is easier than exercise as I still schedule swim time. I find this gives me a happy goal to work toward, but it also allows me to answer honestly when asked for a meeting after lunch on certain weekdays. Confidently, I say, "I'm sorry, but I'm booked" and then offer an alternative. Of course, I could change it, but I rarely do. My meeting with the pool is an integral part of my health plan—my physical, mental, and emotional health plan—and this is something that keeps me alert and creative for engaging with clients and their writing. Plus, I have found that having a client meeting at another time has never been an issue. So, honor your journaling as part of your day along with the nutrition, exercise, and rest that honor your body; the time that honors your career and friendships; the chores that honor your home; the practices that honor your spirit; and so forth.

Beware! Procrastination makes comparisons and often pits one good thing against another.

Your pet needs you. And what about your sweet neighbor? You want to journal by yourself when you should spend time with them?

Answer Never Mind's grumbles with a written affirmation in your journal, a firm inner voice from your commitment, or both. Take small steps and make adjustments until you feel balanced with choosing yourself while still meeting other commitments.

This occurred at similar times for Tay and Ash. Both were committed to career, pets, and community alongside their journaling practice with different results.

"How's your journaling, Tay?" I asked.

"Why did I let them rope me into joining the HOA? The hours *that* takes! And my puppy, Stark, isn't housetrained yet, my folks still expect me to visit a lot, and I never get a good night's sleep."

Ever dutiful, Tay seemed to have fallen into a pattern of not making time for self-care. These omissions included journaling.

"Well, what about your practice—?"

"Everything else is—Oh! My boss threw *another* wrench in my plans," Tay snapped. "Nary a thanks for doing the work of two people."

"Have you written about it? Maybe your journaling can clarify—"

"Oh, I am clear! I hate myself for it!" Looking down, Tay fell silent, then quietly continued. "And I think about journaling. I really do. Heck, sometimes thinking about writing

wakes me up at night. I'll get to it when things slow down…
one of these days."

Truly, "thinking about writing" isn't writing, and "one of
these days" never comes, but know it's okay *not* to journal.
Berating yourself doesn't help. While it's possible for any of us
to get unbalanced with our responsibilities, it often makes it
worse when we beat up or neglect ourselves. Accept the facts
of the situation and shift your commitment from journaling to
finding the time to journal. This may be having a moment of
consideration before bedtime or with Sunday morning coffee
to spot a chance to write a few words. Even if in teeny-tiny
ways—like a small slice of time acquired when you can't sleep
in the middle of the night—the sooner the better. Perhaps that
time will relieve some tension, spark some ideas for easing the
burden, or at least boost you by giving yourself a pat on the
back when others may not be doing so.

While writing was missing in action from Tay's activities, just underneath the venting was a whisper of yearning.
Conversely, Ash has an easy, pragmatic approach, using creativity to mine slivers of time to write.

"I'm overwhelmed with holiday plans," Ash shared, "and
my own party aside, I have other occasions which require a
gift. And it's crazy how competitive the neighborhood cookie
swap has gotten, even worse than the agility trials that Plum
and I compete in every three weeks. And with a freeze on
vacation time at the company, I'm maxed out."

Before I could ask, I got my answer.

"But I squeaked in ten minutes of journaling while I was getting Plum calmed down the other night. She's full grown, twenty pounds but still a puppy. I called her up on the sofa, pulling her belly-up next to me, then balanced a notebook on my lap. Rubbing her tummy with one hand as I scribbled with the other, my words were practically illegible, but I can read them. I gotta journal whenever I can."

I smiled thinking of how Ash created an opportunity and was rewarded with two times the love. What a wonderful way to exercise physical agility and masterful creativity.

"So, I splurged to have gifts wrapped before they were shipped. When they arrived, I pulled them out of the box and admired how great they looked, and then I popped some store-bought cookie dough in the oven. While they baked, I gave Plum a bone, so I could sit with a cup of tea and my journal. Writing re-energized me, and then I was in the spirit to decorate the cookies. Who cares if I lose the cookie competition? I won the afternoon! And oh—" Ash handed me a tin. "Happy Holidays!"

"Thanks!"

Ash keeps the flame of imagination fired up to illuminate challenges and find their simple solutions, bringing balance to life. To Ash, every day is a holiday as every day is a group of moments ripe with opportunities to create. This includes honoring a commitment to a valued journaling practice. Ash exemplifies how we can stoke love to celebrate others by first celebrating ourselves.

Like Tay, Ash, and many other people, journalers have lots to do during waking hours. If you have other plates spinning in the air—career, partner, kiddos, pets, family, friends, house, neighbors, exercise, volunteering, and affiliations, as well as routines in cooking, Pilates, and binging TV shows—does journaling deserve a stick of its own? Can you keep your writing practice spinning by readjusting the speed of the other plates, maybe by shrinking their individual sizes? Or might the time be right to delegate responsibilities elsewhere or even let something go?

If you feel that so much time has passed and you've lost your practice, forgive yourself. Life changes, and commitments do too. If journaling is important to you, consider a commitment checkup. Reflect on what you have created, glancing at the number of pages you've amassed, and mourn its loss, if needed, then realize you can revive it. Feel the pain and then fashion a plan to re-energize it into something good for you now. And start fresh.

If it's simply about restarting a commitment on how often to write, consider "Remember That September." Set a short-term goal to entice a longer-term goal as a renewal exercise for rebuilding commitment. Maybe you need to shake up the place where you journal, so take off for a quick Me Party. And wherever you are, be happy with whatever you write, even if you just make a brief list. When you finish, feel the gratitude and say, "Good journaling!" No matter the scope of the words on the page, stay realistic and positive in rejuvenating your habit. Notice you are already succeeding in recommitment. Now, imagine the next step and take it.

Know that, unlike the farfetched hysteria surrounding Y2K, your fears may be justified. Yes, journaling involves opening to self, and you may fear discovering what you have repressed. As you explore in your written words, it's possible to unearth new revelations and thus provoke the sharp-tongued snaps from Never Mind. Arising from unsought memories or trauma, these shrieks may hit a nerve, making you too afraid to write. Never Mind may also taunt this exposed secret in a way to keep you from journaling altogether. This can happen to anyone at any time in their practice.

When this happens to me, I know to try my best to face it by venturing deep in my journal. I also remember that to grow, I have to accept that my life will change. And Never Mind's taunts and tricks will likely grow and change too.

As Never Mind ramps up the fear, trying to get me to again suppress another thought under the guise of self-protection, this often arrives cloaked in the form of procrastination. Truly, I have also experienced a tag team effort by my own perfection and procrastination as they feed off one another. Perfectionism and its stringent boundaries set off procrastination and its cavalcade of excuses, and then send it back to perfectionism.

Journaling has to be perfect, so try again tomorrow.

This, in turn, leads to:

Relax and rest. Take a nap. Play video games. Skip journaling because it won't be perfect anyway.

And the smackdown from both sides continues until I find my affirmative voice and advance to the page.

Venturing deep is not unlike any other challenge since you may not know what you will discover. This self-exposure can be scary, but remember you are created of creativity to be creative. Life is a time to learn and grow. First, write Never Mind's rants and then shift each into their opposite to affirm your new good. Next, inquire in your journal, writing questions about the specifics of the fear, what you know of it, how you act from it, and how it impacts your feelings. Be steadfast and brave, and you not only open the channel for more memories, but you also discern more about your emotions, thoughts, beliefs, and actions as you write in your journal. If any of the fears or realizations are difficult to handle, turn to your trusted ones for guidance. Seek out those with whom you can share: family, friends, a support group, and the like, or a therapist if you need more objectivity and neutrality with someone who you trust to keep you story private. And consider that your journal remains reliable as you continue to seek and support your growth during this stage and beyond. At every step, be thankful.

My fears around Y2K felt like a reaction to the blistering, years-long media blitz. Though I tried to keep up with the news, I simultaneously dodged the negative stories, and both actions left me fatigued. My plan to live through this apocalyptic nightmare seemed logical, but most of my actions were like those on New Year's Eve when I figured that if I took a swim, cooked comfort food, and saw friends as if everything was fine, it would all go away. At that time, this was as positive as I could be. I was really procrastinating any effort to get involved or to uncover the truth in the media muck, much less utilize this to fortify my peace. Instead of grounding in affirmation, I practiced denial. Yet, as soon as the crucial moment safely passed and years after catching my breath, I discovered there was more to my fear than that one occurrence. Some 13 years into my daily practice, I realized my knee-jerk reactions emboldened victimhood instead of using creativity for thoughtful responses to take ownership of my life.

Journaled words over time revealed this dread had been with me as long as I could remember. I had to look more closely at my fear of death from childhood when, somehow from somewhere or someone, I accepted a belief that I was flawed at birth, not worthy to live, even the one who deserved the blame. This fear exploded, mushrooming over me through other incidents, most vividly during major life changes and personal losses, as well as through the AIDS Epidemic, the 9/11 terrorist attacks, and the Covid-19 Pandemic.

When anxiety spins out of control until Never Mind stamps it "unresolved," I accept that's that, and the fog of depression descends, followed by physical and emotional exhaustion. With my journal's companionship and my trusted ones' support, I have made headway by accepting the fact of physical death while improving practices of self-care. This shifts what I think and do into the Now, leading me to a better place emotionally. And I am coming to terms with my habit of worrying by holding a new truth that being creative uses that same energy in a positive way while lifting me up.

Worry invalidates affirmation. Therefore, I work to remain aware of the perspective in my "what if?" questions. If focused on the past, I usually experience regret. If focused on the future, I usually experience fear. So, when I focus on the present, I use the question "what *is?*" to see the truth of where I am in the moment. Truth allows an honest approach, even when I look back at "what was?" or consider "what might be?"

I also venture to convert my "what if?" questions into positive affirmations. Farfetched at times, poetic at others, I consider how "What if the sky falls?" becomes "What is my life like today?" answering "I breathe and live enthusiastically. If the sky falls, I savor the chance to commune up close with a cloud."

Honestly, at times my affirmed optimism still seems irrational. Fortunately, time-tested affirmations I've written, along with popular wisdom such as "This too will pass" and "One day at a time," help me stay balanced in the moment until I find additional facts and feelings to write more detailed affirmations to live by. Thus far, I am happy I have found a way to live my affirmations through facing my worries, anxieties, and primal fears. And yes, I persist and keep it up.

L ife consistently presents you with choices. As you journal, Never Mind manipulates, blending into the pack of inspired ideas, intuitive guidance, and creative debate in your writer's mind. Growling at and herding away the good to keep you lying low, Never Mind wants you to stay securely in what is known and away from what is not. This way of thinking trades true growth for false safety, which presented by Never Mind makes perfect sense until you feel the boredom and inertia of your life. The sameness isn't necessarily safe, just the same. So, strengthen your positive internal voice as those of procrastination will always be around. Ban what is no longer your truth—even if it was your truth yesterday—and affirm "what is?" by sealing the deal as you write in your journal. Solidify your life path and progress in your practice.

The soothsayers and the naysayers battled it out for media domination leading up to Y2K, building their case on truth while spreading the dramatic hoax to get the world to stop everything and worry. They pontificated about dying to keep everyone from focusing on living.

Procrastination pulls the same slight-of-hand with its broken promises, activating a misuse of the power of creativity. When Never Mind barks doubt, fear, and excuses, don't wait! Stand in your writing spirit and affirm good to release the hounds from your thinking. Be the strong, yet loving caretaker of your time by exercising your journaling practice, remembering every day is a great day to be alive.

9

Procrastination

AFFIRMING A JOURNALER'S CONSCIOUSNESS

Use affirmations, one or all, adapting as desired.

I am grateful for the present moment as I know "one of these days" never comes. My opportunity to journal is right now.

When procrastination growls its deceits and denials to keep me from acting on my passion, I write anyway.

I stop creating excuses, and I exercise my heart's commitment as I journal.

Near me, I arrange all I need to be centered, stay seated, and keep writing.

I change even without making a conscious decision to do so. Now, I choose to be intentional in my choices.

If I come upon a reason not to journal, I write about it, forgive myself, think positively, and move forward.

Writing is one word at a time. I take the first step, starting where I am.

Always satisfying a worthy purpose, my journaling is a favored practice in my daily life.

When imbalanced, I shift my commitment from the writing itself to finding the time to write. Once I do, I journal.

Life is a time to learn and grow. This knowledge provides vital energy and influences my personal writing.

I slow to savor the flavor of solace in a taste of gratitude.

Procrastination is a broken promise to my spirit and a misuse of creativity. Aware, I gratefully focus and spend time journaling.

Write an affirmation about overpowering procrastination.

- Begin with either "I am…" or "I…" followed by an action verb in present tense, such as revive, manage, or swallow.
- Complete with heartfelt words to lift your spirit and motivate your growth.

9

Procrastination

PROMPTING A JOURNALER'S PRACTICE

Choose a word or phrase,
and then journal what comes up.

○ Resolution

○ Procrastination's distractions

Complete the sentence and write more.

○ "Journaling encourages my creativity by…"

Create your own prompt and journal from it.

○

10

Writing Dreams

My visions
when I am asleep
sharpen my awareness,
strengthen my journaling, and
support my growth
when I am awake.

WORM SPAGHETTI
WITH A WEED SALAD SIDE

"Are you looking for bubbles?" I asked, interrupting our discussion about dreams. "Because I don't see any."

Roberta and I peered into the sealed plastic cup that held her Thai bubble tea. Having never witnessed this drink before, I had imagined an effervescent concoction from a mad scientist's lab or something theatrical like a Flaming Volcano, not just a beverage but an event.

"No, I'm looking for tapioca," Roberta snapped. "I loathe tapioca."

"Why?"

She abruptly set the cup on the table and glared at me. "Tapioca is like gummy bear turds."

I grinned and noted her declaration in the back of my journaler's mind as she stabbed the tea's lid with a straw, then took a hearty, tapioca-turd-free gulp before calmly returning to the subject at hand.

"Most people are horrified of exploring their subconscious." As a budding therapist, Roberta was always enthusiastic to analyze human behavior. "So, what gave you such a comfortable relationship with yours?"

I pursed my lips as I considered. "The combination of nightmares in early childhood, then being told by my dad that they were mine and I could change them. So, I began to look at dreams more closely."

She sipped her tea and looked at me with a slight nod and an eyebrow lift that close friends and some therapists do to signal "go on."

"Just like I remember nursery rhymes, I remember dreams I had when I was about three or four—"

"You remember a dream from when you were three years old?!" she exclaimed from friend mode.

"Yeah…or four. Don't you?"

With neither a nod nor an eyebrow lift, she maintained her gaze and sipped, thus evading the question by returning to all-ears therapist mode.

"I dreamed I was riding on the interstate in the back seat of the family Pontiac. I was looking out the window at an army of men on lawn tractors, cutting grass up a steep hill. Suddenly, one of the mowers flipped over backwards, crushing its rider, then another flipped and another. I woke up terrified."

"Then what?"

"I ran to get my dad, or he heard me cry out and came in to lie next to me on my bed until I went back to sleep. That's when he told me that they are my dreams and I can change them."

"Just like ordering from a menu," she said, cradling her cup in both hands.

"Or ordering *off* the menu."

On cue, the waiter arrived to take our order. I decided to step outside my comfort zone with a dish unknown beyond the word "noodles."

"So, were you afraid of the dark?"

"Petrified," I said. "More than the eerie TV shows *The Outer Limits* and *The Twilight Zone* keeping me awake, it was the relentless teasing and premeditated frights I got from other kids. Alone in my bedroom with my stuffed animals and a nightlight on, I saw flashes of color and felt there were beings in the shadows. Of course, I imagined they were the Boogeyman or ravenous monsters."

Roberta slurped then shook the ice in the cup as I sipped water and went on.

"Around that time, I had a dream where I was in my neighbors' backyard, and three of us kids were playing. The game was 'cooking dinner,' so I was making a salad from all kinds of weeds I picked in the woods up the hill where I could look through a fence down upon the earth movers building I-285."

"The interstate again?" she pondered aloud.

"Uh-huh, and this one under construction and from a different viewpoint, above instead of below. So, on the patio, I shared my part of the meal, and one kid made me mad when she suddenly changed the rules. I didn't want to play anymore, so I threw the salad onto the concrete and ran to the front yard, feeling all dejected, my pouty lip poking out, when suddenly I saw this huge head over the rooftop." I paused for effect and leaned across the table. "Then there he was in front of me, a twenty-five-foot-tall man who was completely blue, both his skin and clothes, even the whites of his eyes, as if only the outlines existed and some kid colored him slightly darker than the sky."

"Wow," she said flatly, then after a loud slurp, asked, "Did you wake up?"

"No. I freaked out, then immediately remembered that this was a dream, and since it was mine, I could change it. Without saying a word, I wished in my mind that the colossal blue man was little. He instantly shrunk to my size, I ran over to him, and we began to play."

The waiter arrived with our food as I continued. "I know my subconscious is just that. It's mine, so I can change it, even direct it. It comes to me full-on each night and brings me even more messages every day," I stated emphatically before my attention was grabbed by the delicious aroma from the strange tubular noodles on the plate. I looked back up as I unwrapped my silverware. "Why would I be afraid of my subconscious? It's part of who I am, a space filled with ideas, images, intuitions, and remembrances from my entire life."

Roberta grunted affirmatively as she chewed.

"Still, I wonder why certain dreams come at certain times. I've breathed underwater and dove into the depths of imagination. Do I somehow choose images and events like songs for a playlist, or is it more like hitting shuffle on my MP3 player? Some are obviously experiences I've had, yet some seem so new."

I tried to wrap my noodles around a fork like spaghetti, but they were thick and slippery like rubber fishing worms. I formulated a new plan as Roberta easily devoured her normal noodles.

"What I *do* know is that dreams offer me a chance to discover more about myself through visuals and language that relate to my life...like movies made just for me."

Talking about dreams over food felt natural since I began the practice at the breakfast table as a kid. My mother often wondered what she'd fed me the previous night as if I was like Scrooge who believed his ghostly visions on Christmas Eve were caused by a bit of bad beef. Since Dad usually headed to work before I finished my scrambled eggs or oatmeal, dream talk could spill over to supper. Dreams were treated as another part of life, or maybe my parents humored my fascination. For me, aside from my frights, there was out-of-this-world magic and puzzling riddles in this nightly experience that was both personal and fun.

Probing my interest in dreams was the primary reason I started journaling daily on my first computer in the late '80s. Soon, I began to study the narrative and imagery while beginning to understand the correlation between my waking and sleeping lives. I had learned many feel that what happened in their previous day shows up in their dreams, yet I began to also see how my dreams foreshadowed what was to come.

Unlike the clandestine synchronicities and clammy-skin feelings of déjà vu, I recalled the symbols and occurrences from my dream in the moment they mirrored my life.

As I began to be challenged by financial struggles, personality conflicts, unsatisfying romances, and frightening realities, waking life seemed more nightmarish than any bad dream, and I felt I could use all the help I could get. Whereas on occasion at night I could make a decision and change the course of the dream's narrative, it would be sometime before I realized that changing the way I think during waking times and affirming good could do the same thing in my everyday life.

Through my journaling, I started to believe that the conscious interactions of day and the subconscious interactions of night were intertwined. What I could understand was that I was not only learning from my dreams, but I was entertained and comforted by them, just like what happened to me as a child. Journeying into sleep was welcomed, even idyllic, so I began to recognize that perhaps all of life—every breath, every thought, every action—could be peaceful too. In my writing, questions brought answers which often led to more questions in a committed rotation of observance, inquiry, and realization.

I believe dreams are a different kind of personal reality. Their messages are rarely straightforward, often told through metaphor or mystery. This may seem odd but consider how many times in your "real" life you are confronted by having to unravel the truth of what is being said or shown to you. Is there really that much of a difference? Consider how often you reminisce on the good ole days or the hard times of yesteryear, or you flash forward into romantic notions or terrifying scenarios? Though thoughts of past and future, these happen in the present. With either recollection or speculation—whether positive or negative—your heart pumps, your lungs take in air, and you are fully alive in them. Dreams, like waking life's moments, are real and present-oriented with every beat and every breath.

Dreams sometime seem like a mishmash of memories. So, do dreams display messages where every character represents others in your life, or is every character a reflection of yourself? I look at both sides of this question just as I do in my daytime life where people and actions reflect a situational truth, but also a personal one. This mirroring also happens through journaling as you write what you know, creating an opportunity to learn through the reflection of your words back to you as you write and, later, when you review.

Dream work in journaling can evoke creativity and inspire growth, both beneficial for your practice. Ideas stirred and memories invigorated are gathered, arranged, imagined, and re-imagined in the process of journal writing. This energetic interstate becomes both an open connection, as well as a smoothly paved, beautifully manicured route I am comfortable traveling, making my process faster and more joyful. The subconscious and conscious mind are ever connected, so I use them as one. Both day and night, they offer heightened sensual, intuitive, and creative awareness toward elevated expression and output for my practice.

This was illustrated in a Friday night dream journaled on Saturday morning, July 24, 2010:

> I'm seated in the passenger-side backseat of a
> 1990s black Chrysler LeBaron convertible with
> no driver. Intuitively, I knew to write while
> trusting the vehicle as it rolled down the street
> of some town I didn't recognize. I looked up,
> and the car was staying in the lane, so I went
> back to writing on my laptop, perched on a tray
> table attached to the seat in front of me like
> those found on airplanes. I looked up again as I
> passed a restaurant where a cop and a waitress
> served up cold stares at me in my driverless car. I
> worried about getting arrested but focused hard
> on my writing. When I looked up again, I was
> rolling into a complicated intersection with lots of
> interweaving traffic. More than before, I thought
> of jumping the seat to tap the brakes but knew I
> shouldn't. I didn't want to look away, but the urge
> to keep writing overcame me alongside the desire
> to trust the forward movement. I continued
> to write…

This dream affirmed I was not just moving forward with my writing, but I was being inspired as long as I didn't let fear break my trust. By remaining focused on creativity and the flow forward, I stood strong against Never Mind's threats for me to jump into worry. As I typed, I also noticed the play on words with the waitress and cop "serving up" fear of my progress "being arrested," as well as "braking" the car and "breaking" my trust. The mind, both what the subconscious delivers and the conscious interprets, is awesome.

I consider every dream, fragment, and symbol that I recall. Similar to how the choice of a writing prompt is made by the energy I feel from it, I allow my intuition to guide me to those parts of a dream that deserve first attention. When journaling, I often feel the emotional charge alerting me to one for deeper inquiry. From the onset of nightmares at an early age to the discussion around meals at the family table, I have trained myself to stay in shape to capture and ponder these messages.

Dream work to create the subconscious/conscious connection is important for journalers in getting skilled at having contact with this "other world." Dreams can float away quickly when not given attention and noted. Similarly, thoughts, memories, and ideas for journal entries can quickly vanish from the forefront of consciousness back into subconscious depths when they reveal at inopportune moments like when driving, showering, exercising, conversing, and so forth. Both can make you think, "Where did that come from?" as well as "Where did that go?" With dreams, affirm your desire, be alert to its manifestation, and as soon as possible, record this inspiration and be grateful for it. Write the raw dream down before your mind can evaluate or censor, much less dismiss or forget it. Pull your focus back across the border to the subconscious before the accelerating thinking mind hurls you into the bustling streets of consciousness. Even if you can just helicopter above your wide-awake thoughts to view the vista "over there," do it and capture all you see within the words of your journal. And when in your day, do the same for unexpected inspiration arriving at inconvenient times.

To support my early commitment to journaling my dreams, I kept a pad and pen by the bed to net nightly visions. In a similar way I scrawl intriguing notes when in the car at a traffic light, I pinpoint a word or short phrase that will remind me of what I experienced in my recent dream. This takes practice, and I learned not to get frustrated if I couldn't access the dream from what had been written. I also let it go if I couldn't read my handwriting or had inadvertently written one note over another in the dark. Beyond that, I also forgave myself for the time I wrote on my sheets, celebrating a permanent bedtime reminder of a dream I snagged and wrote in my journal.

During this process, I began to remember an average of three dreams each night. One night I remembered five, other nights none. I learned to release negativity and even congratulate myself if I tried but couldn't remember the dream. Eventually, I aimed to remain on the border between conscious and subconscious awareness, delivering dream details into consciousness while holding off other thoughts, like the day's to-do list or Never Mind's morning worries. This worked some of the time. I journaled each dream with every detail I could recall, even taking all senses into account, which led to developed awareness beyond sight and hearing to smell, touch, and taste within some dreams.

I stopped the harmful habit of calling my dreams "crazy." Like an experimental film or some forms of jazz music, I view them as non-linear with a story beneath these scattered images, sounds, and feelings. All dreams are quite sane.

I knew a guy who vehemently denied dreaming. Maybe he really didn't as there are reasons why some don't, including irregular sleep patterns. Still, I offered the possibility that he just doesn't remember them. Considering how such a pessimistic statement guides the subconscious, he probably never will dream since his belief negates any opportunity. The subconscious expression will not happen or will be cut off at the border of waking, and he will miss out on the experience. For those who feel the same, I suggest affirming an openness to the discovery of dreaming upon awakening, receiving with gratitude, journaling about it, then expanding awareness by asking for more.

Once you have a dream or fragments you recall, you can journey to discover what meanings it holds. There are as many definitions of dream symbols as there are dreams. As you ponder the symbols—the dark staircase, the chatty daffodil, the plunging elevator, the ancestor standing silently by your side, the light switch you can't quite reach—pay attention to what quickly comes to mind around them. Though you can seek guidance from books, therapists, and friends, the final answer relies on your intuition, thoughts, and emotions. You'll know by an "a-ha" or a positive feeling. Additionally, a symbol's meaning can change from dream to dream since the dream is of you, and you are always growing.

Truly the dream's message is a personal puzzle to piece together. After journaling the dream, I often write ideas and interpretations before moving into journaling about waking life. Approach this with playfulness and wonder, not like it's a research project. Blend your mental acuity and creative savvy. Remember, too, other ideas may come to mind throughout the day or even through other dreams at night. For example, the blue man from my childhood dream felt like the hidden anger of being different and the fear that I never would belong. These feelings followed me around. Perhaps the dream gave me a chance to see the situation anew, to play with it, to find ways to cope and stay safe. The interpretation has morphed over the years as my awareness amplified, both for me as an adult looking back, as well as for the inner child who still sees and feels the dream's immediate presence.

Some dreams have many meanings. I had a dream where I encountered three hawks and an owl, all standing in a row on pebbles in a flower bed. I pondered what the predatory birds symbolized as day and night visionaries, also considering how they hunt. I felt this image was about an imbalance in my day and night selves, but then I thought that it might mean something about where I needed more protection, perhaps three times as much in the day than at night. I allowed all meanings to keep my mind open to assorted paths. The imagery was so striking that it continues to influence me like a renowned painting created in my subconscious, suddenly spotlighted in the gallery of consciousness. Whenever the image resurfaces, I pay attention.

If a dream symbol stumps you but you are still intrigued, write down whatever you can, even if the ideas are "around" the symbol. Consider ruminating on a dream symbol, whether it's a person, a situation, an emotion, even a color. Dialogue with this feature in writing to see what else you can discover. Be grateful as you've valued yourself and the dream by writing it down; now, ponder it without obsessing. And as you are preparing to go to sleep, affirm that your subconscious delivers clarity and then remain grateful for whatever comes.

When you establish recall and practice dream journaling, notice where you are within the dream. What is your point of view? Are you participating as a player in the scene? Are you watching from the side or from above, at a distance like watching a movie in a darkened theater, or are you within the dream, hiding like a voyeur or standing in plain sight like an eavesdropper? Do you have multiple vantage points? What do these points of view expose in light of the content?

I remember hearing that if you dreamed of seeing yourself in a mirror, you would die just like you would if you dreamed of falling off a cliff and hit bottom. I have had both occur, and so far, I lived to journal about them. For example, when I reached the bottom of the cliff, my dream simply changed.

In one dream when I looked into a mirror, I saw my glasses had an additional lens centered on the frames above my nose. As I kept looking into the mirror, I demanded to see the "real" eye doctor, horrified at how these glasses made me look. I woke with a smile, easily recognizing the symbology of the extra lens on top to magnify the power of my third eye. It was as if this mystical spot on my forehead where I receive mental perception beyond ordinary sight, such as images in dreams and intuitive visions, was a "real" human eyeball which looked inward, not outward. Obviously, I was getting the "real" doctor's help through the dream's magnification of my awareness in the power of my third eye, but I wasn't ready to believe that I could do anything with it because I had yet to receive the gift. The added lens and its vision were something ugly, something to reject. My vanity of who I thought I was or should be stood in the way of my growth.

Are you less of a dreamer if your night movies are in black and white rather than Technicolor? I don't believe so. Within the spectrum of color or shades of gray, ask yourself if there is significance in these aspects shown in your dream and what they say to you. Notice how a room is furnished, the dullness or vividness of the horizon, even the clothes the people wear. If you dream in grayscale and want to dream in color or vice versa, ask for it, be aware of its presence, and be grateful when it appears.

From my personal experience, nightmares come with a jolt of fear from failure to heed previous messages about their subject. Most likely, I have been shown variations on this theme from my subconscious at night as well as reflected to me in my daily life. This added spike of scary energy is my subconscious forcefully getting my attention. Fear often has roots of guilt, shame, trauma, and so much more in a concoction stirred from a single incident or a lifetime of occurrences. The wound that scabbed over, allowing me to function or maybe to survive, re-opens to let out the infection.

With a nightmare's literal "wake-up call," perhaps your spirit knows you're ready to look at this fear. It's possible you've supported your growth enough to make this a safe time. Though how you got to this point is likely in the words of your journal, be present and use the dream as the catalyst to write the depth of its detail. Be grateful for its surfacing and take good self-care—perhaps with added guidance from your most trusted ones—as you bravely make your way to compassionate growth.

When fear wakes you, make sure you're okay, and then catch your breath, affirm your safety, and write the details and emotions surrounding the fear. From your initial nighttime notes and multiple entries, let the bigger picture and every frayed edge appear. Rely on your practice as you authentically journal this incident, then go to your heart, mind, and spirit for additional realizations. Remember, writing fear's messages is a step to shifting your limited beliefs. Honor this with affirmations to find forgiveness for self and others, to heal wounds, and to shift behaviors for more freedom in your life and your dreams.

As an adult, the frequency of my nightmares greatly decreased. Some disturbing dreams require going through the house, turning on lights, and checking the locks before making my way to the desk to notate details. For others, I grab the pad from my nightstand and jot snippets in the dark. By continually acknowledging and exploring these dreams, I feel this hinders the fear from escalation as it did earlier in my life. With the details of the scary dream notated and put away, I snuggle under the covers and affirm ease in getting back to sleep with a peaceful mind, then I focus on my breath going in and out, in and out...

Some dreams or dream symbols recur. I recognize places I have visited in dreams time after time, but I have no conscious recall of their Earthly existence. Perhaps the images are more of those paintings on loan from my subconscious, or maybe from a vault hidden in my unconscious mind. Still, I find it interesting how they show up the same in multiple dreams. They often involve bodies of water and miles of blue skies, places evoking passionate appeal. Their sensual gift of freedom conjures a primal experience which can swiftly shift to a vast, enveloping fear:

> I'm standing on a narrow, floating dock-like structure made of 4' x 4' shipping pallets bound together. This stretches into a wide expanse of a calm bay close to an ocean. With each step to the end, another pallet surfaces and attaches, and I keep moving. At the water's midpoint between shores, the sky darkens, choppy waves rise, and the dock pitches. With no railing for security, I drop to my hands and knees. I am too far out to go back, and with my sudden immobility, the dock doesn't add pallets for me to crawl to the distant bank. As the wind howls, the waves intensify, violently thrashing the wooden structure, threatening to rip it apart as I desperately hang on—

Waking abruptly, I wrote the details. I easily recognized the symbol about choice and movement through potent fear, asking what emotion was tossing me about or what I was clutching to remain stuck in dangerous tides. I looked closely at my life, examining it through that dynamic dream scene. I received more than one answer, and I took action, offering affirmation on the observation with the most power in the moment. With this dream recurring, the exercise is repeated, and each time, the guidance through my practice brings either an answer in a different shade from before or one of a completely different stripe. I stay open and grateful as I write.

At times, I am aware of my thinking and decision-making during the dream. Lucid dreaming offers me the power of choice within my subconscious like I did as a child with the blue man dream. Usually, this is when I float off the ground and fly. Someone once shared an exercise to help me get to this level of awareness: stop and focus on your hand, your wrist, or your foot during waking time, asking aloud, "Am I dreaming?" and answer while focused. Perhaps some night, you will do this in a dream and reach that place of lucidity—of conscious presence—within your subconscious. Here, you can make choices of subjects, details, and interactions.

At other times, I levitate in my dreams and have also swam underwater as fast as I could fly above it, once doing both in succession. I figure skate, too, a feat I find graceful, but one I attempted in my teens, resulting in multiple spills. In dreams, most of my jumps become an expansive flying, spinning leap. Sometimes when I realize I'm flying, especially if I have any doubt, I safely float back to the ground and then feel irritable as I wake up.

In a similar way I work with affirmations during my day to reprogram the fearful demands of Never Mind, I experiment with the use of lucidity in dreaming to set intentions. Where better than in your dreams to plant positive intentions firmly in the subconscious? Just like you can recognize your lucidity in a dream and make the instant choice to fly, you can choose to set an intention for love, prosperity, health, or anything else you desire to bring good to your life. Affirming direction in dreamtime puts the thought in subconscious mind for the "dreaming up" of more good. Consider, too, when you trust that the good already exists in your thoughts and is coming to you, your changed thinking makes you more aware of opportunities and the creativity needed to reach that goal. Now, imagine your conscious and subconscious teamed up. Ah, a dream come true.

Since we are creating and living in both dreaming and waking worlds, they often seem very similar. Consider this:

> At nightfall, I am driving on a four-lane highway
> as traffic moves in unison. Suddenly, I'm above it
> and see the patterns of the red taillights coming
> on in succession toward me. When grounded
> and moving again, I notice a vintage Rolls Royce
> waiting to merge from a dirt road alongside
> a pond. Next, I'm behind a school bus. The

conventional yellow paint surrounds a gloomy
back window. I think it's reflective, but then I
see something moving inside. Is it a child? No,
it's E.T. the Extra Terrestrial looking at me. He
fades back into the darkness. I see the side of
his face, then his frontal view, then he vanishes
again. I stop at a traffic light, and a massive,
red tow truck muscles alongside me. It's so high
above my car that I can't see the driver, then I
anxiously realize I have to move across several
lanes to get on the interstate...

Though dreamlike, this was observed and journaled in
real life. It begs the question, "What is reality anyway?" No,
I did not float out of my car, but on this unexplored stretch
of dark highway, I crested a hill, viewing traffic spreading out
below me for over a mile, seizing my attention. Enhanced by
my car stereo blaring an impromptu soundtrack, the scene was
glorious. The Rolls Royce was as real as the red wrecker. Once
getting the light shining on it from another vehicle, I realized
E.T. was a Mylar balloon jostling around while tethered to
a seat on the bus. And as irritating as traffic can usually be,
this slow-moving mass took my breath away. So, relax, and
let your imagination and awareness play together.

Almost everyone, particularly writers, searches for symbols
and interprets signs in their lives, in the books they read, in
the films and broadcasts they watch or hear, in both fiction

and nonfiction, even in the people they meet, so why not in dreams? Wake up to dreams as part of one reality, just delivered in a unique way. Dreams can be your guide to sweeping creativity, the heightened awareness to catch it, and the words to journal it with your writing spirit.

Your dreams can be a trusted companion like Roberta, who serves a very mature honesty alongside a childlike wonder when we get together. No matter the topic, time obviously passes, yet time doesn't seem to exist. She is both observant and analytical like a good therapist, as well as creative and caring like a revered friend, mirroring life's waking and dream-filled moments.

Soon after my discussion with Roberta over noodles, I visited my parents. My 82-year-old dad stirred beef stew on the stove while Mom, in the latter stages of Parkinson's disease, sat expressionless, obsessively pulling tissues slowly from their box and then gently tearing them into pieces.

I felt glad my parents' home was serene. I had long observed Dad's vibrant creativity and steadfast fortitude as he moved mountains to bring her comfort. All he would accept was my encouragement and gratitude as I truly believed the good he'd given had added years to Mom's life. Still, try as he might, he couldn't engineer a path to rescue his beloved from her illness, and his eyes couldn't hide his sorrow.

At the kitchen table, Mom quietly resisted Dad's attempts to feed her, and he remained patiently attentive while conversing with me. Living this nightmare in waking time, I bowed my head toward the bowl of stew and inhaled the steamy aroma, attempting to echo Dad's stoicism. I put aside my heartbreak for his loss, my heartbreak for my loss in knowing that Mom was not long for this world, and my heartbreak for her loss that neither he nor I could comprehend. I placed these feelings just outside my present thinking, not to dismiss them into the depth of my subconscious, but to hold them for the next morning's journaling when I could lay them down, look them over in private, and begin to see another step to support and grieve. As I brought a spoonful to my mouth, I purposefully affirmed strength, filling my thoughts with the light of gratitude that we were all still here, a loving family just as we'd been for decades, around this table on this day.

To lighten the mood, I mentioned my recent dream chat with Roberta, then I shared about the nightmares I had as a kid. Dad recalled that happening. Since we'd never talked about it, I took this time to show my appreciation for his care when I was a little boy.

"Thank you, Dad, for lying next to me on my bed in the middle of the night when I was scared after a bad dream, telling me that it was my dream and I could change it if I wanted to."

He swallowed then looked me in the eye, smiling with the sincerity I'd treasured my whole life, and said, "I didn't do that."

Chills rushed throughout my body. All these years, I had clung to the belief that it was my father next to me, protecting and calming me, giving guidance in the dark, and those beings in the misty shadows were just a dream. Perhaps they were watchful elders visible only as subtle shapes behind a gauzy veil of aquamarine, pink, and gold which twinkled with energetic bursts like distant stars in the night sky. And maybe they lulled me back to sleep while Dad got some shut-eye across the hall. Or could I have gotten it all mixed up? Was I lucid in my subconscious, or was the whole experience just me dreaming another dream?

"You didn't?" I asked.

"Nope," he said, raising a platter toward me. "Want some more cornbread?"

Taking a piece and crumbling it into my stew, I looked at Mom, my blank stare meeting hers. I pondered that both physical, eyes-opened, everyday vision and non-physical, third-eye, inner vision blend to make the reality of my life. With my commitment to journaling's flow through my subconscious into consciousness, every morsel is nourishing. As I learn something new, more comes into focus.

All in the house hushed except for Mom tugging a fresh tissue and Dad loading another spoonful for her, while in my mind, I heard echoes of my favorite nursery rhyme, the one which serenaded me to sleep throughout childhood. "Merrily, merrily, merrily, merrily, life is but a dream."

10

Dreams

AFFIRMING A JOURNALER'S CONSCIOUSNESS

Use affirmations, one or all, adapting as desired.

Dreams uniquely inspire my personal growth and guide my evolution as a journal writer.

Dreamtime, like awake time, is real and alive with every breath.

I grow comfortable with my subconscious. Each night and every day, it delivers ideas and inspiration. I value it as a vital part of my life and journaling practice.

I capture dreams by affirming this desire before I fall asleep, then awakening, remembering, and writing it down.

My dreams are non-linear, uniquely my own, and quite sane.

I search for symbols and interpret signs in my daily life and nightly dreams. I write about it all.

I train myself to wake with a clear mind, remaining between subconscious and conscious awareness to hold on to my dream until I journal the details.

If a nightmare wakes me, I affirm my safety and write the experience, knowing fear offers a path to growth.

A deeper meaning, even multiple meanings, are found through the mirroring of my dreams, my life, and my journaling.

I am aware of my presence in a lucid dream, granting conscious choice within my subconscious. I write the specifics.

I integrate my dreaming life alongside my waking life and into my writing life.

Journaling is a dream come true.

Write an affirmation about exploring dreams.

- ○ Begin with either "I am…" or "I…" followed by an action verb in present tense, such as reminisce, pinpoint, or symbolize.
- ○ Complete with heartfelt words to lift your spirit and motivate your growth.

10

Dreams

PROMPTING A JOURNALER'S PRACTICE

Choose a word or phrase,
and then journal what comes up.

o   Color or black and white

o   Recurring

Complete the sentence and write more.

o   "My waking and sleeping lives intertwine…"

Create your own prompt and journal from it.

o

11

Writing
Reflection

My journal's words
mirror my truth,
and
I respect this gift
through wise review
and continued writing.

I Am an Open Book

"**G**ood morning. Please come in."

Her words wafted just above the noise from the babbling brook which had captured my attention while waiting for her to unlock the building. I joined the others who were about to paint with Melody's guidance.

I had journaled that morning about feeling honored to be invited into her studio, the inner sanctum where she explored her conscious and subconscious through art. I knew from friends who'd recommended her that she had painted throughout her life, but rare few—mostly teachers and fellow painters—had ever viewed her work. No one had critiqued the finished product. The only discussion was about the process itself.

Following her down the high-ceilinged hallway of this one-time elementary school, I noticed her braided mane of red hair which fell to her waist. Filing into the classroom, the wall of windows framed a view of a magical mountain miles across a verdant valley. The only furnishings were a worn leather sofa and a few mismatched chairs. I assumed Melody's supplies were in the adjacent teacher's storage closet. Other than the original chalkboards, nothing, including her paintings, decorated the walls.

The pristine space held a ring of easels which circled a long, thin table with a few dozen plastic cups filled with paints, the spectrum arranged by color in a pair of parallel rows. All were vivid, even the gray and the flesh tone. The brown looked luscious enough for dipping strawberries. The yellow-green mimicked the color of leaves budding in spring. The tempera paints, though standard school supplies, were especially inviting. And like utensils on a buffet, containers of brushes in various sizes and shapes flanked each end alongside bowls of water.

While awaiting instruction, I stared at the easel's large sheet of crisp white paper. My gut seethed with a mixture of desire and dread.

"Feel what attracts you and follow it," she offered, her genuine smile shining through her cosmetics free face. "Choose a brush that speaks to you, dip it in the color you are drawn to, then put the paint on the paper in the way that feels best."

My classmates and I, all middle-aged, excitedly looked at each other, then I stifled a nervous giggle.

Melody grinned, adding, "As you focus on your process, please don't comment on someone's painting, even to give a compliment."

As the others eagerly grabbed brushes, I held back, maintaining a hesitant fake-smile while feelings of loss and inadequacy enveloped me. I had taken only one art class, and this was with my best friend, an avid painter at ten years old. I was strictly a crayon and marker user. The oil paints, even holding a brush, were foreign to me, plus there was stinky linseed oil and turpentine for paint thinner and brush cleaner. In Mr. Booth's class surrounded by his award-winning paintings, I could feel the reverence for the teacher, a nationally known painter who lived in a little town nearby. I listened to his lengthy, confusing instruction, then I began painting a landscape from a photo he'd ripped out of a magazine.

The teacher walked around the room, addressing each student one by one. After praising my friend on his art, Mr. Booth stepped behind me, sighing heavily before reaching over my shoulder with his thick, hairy arm to take the brush from my small hand. He never made eye contact or said a word as he demonstrated how to enliven the field of wheat, blend the colors, and create shadow and movement. After handing the brush back to me and moving on, I tried, but my attempts were no comparison to the teacher's brushstrokes on my canvas. I glanced over at my friend's lovely painting and felt doomed to failure, guilty that I had wasted my parents' money on costly supplies and lessons. I knew I wouldn't produce a painting that could be framed and displayed, only more shame-inducing interactions. Affirming my hopeless lack of talent on the ride home, I created an excuse and quit the class, hiding my painting, supplies, and guilt in the back of the closet until years later when I could throw out the dried-up tubes and bury the painful memories.

For decades, Mr. Booth's forearm was a character in my Never Mind as I flashed back to that horrific scene whenever around paintings or artists. And I never touched another paintbrush…until now.

As the others vigorously put colors on the paper, Melody noticed my dilemma. She didn't question the past but brought me back to the present.

"So, what brush do you like?"

Still stuck in my worries, I pointed to one of medium girth. "Maybe this, I guess."

"Good."

She nodded toward it, and I picked it up, feeling its weight.

"Now, what color catches your attention?"

"They're all pretty…"

"Pick one," she encouraged with a soft smile.

I carefully dipped my brush into the bright red, wiping the excess on the side of the cup before looking at her for approval. She continued to smile. I held my hand under the brush to avoid a mess as I moved the few feet to my easel. Then I stopped.

"Now," Melody said, "feel free and put the paint where it wants to go."

I touched the wet brush to the paper, and a drop trickled down with gravity's pull, so I felt compelled to follow it. I passed beyond, painting a swerve down the middle, aware of my slight delight before feeling disappointment when the brush went dry. I returned to the paint table, dipping the brush in the familiar red to complete the curvy line. Next, I cleaned the brush in water, wiped it dry, then dipped it in turquoise, adding it to the paper.

As I wondered what this looked like, Melody addressed the class. "Don't consider what you are painting. Just paint."

I cleaned the brush, put it away, then moved to a small fan-shaped brush to satisfy my curiosity of what it would do on the paper. Attracted to another color, then another, then trying another brush, I painted and painted, moving around the paper, playing with color, unconcerned about form, patterns, or really anything other than the fun of putting paint in empty white spaces. The process was all about the paper and the paint, about the connection of hand and brush, about the disconnection from analysis to allow unencumbered creativity and surprising expression. The only goal was to be in the moment and paint.

This process felt easy and comfortable, reminding me of my years of journaling. The brushes represented my fingers, and the array of colors were like the keys on my keyboard. The painted images mirrored my diverse collection of thoughts, feelings, actions, and dreams I put down in words. Just as journaling isn't about writing a bestseller, this painting wasn't about creating a masterpiece. Unlike the expensive oil painting supplies and canvas of my childhood experience, here I used nothing of high cost or foul odor, just a nice-weight vellum and powdered tempera mixed with tap water, comparable to the paper and ink of journaling.

Painting this way also made me think about journaling during the adventure of a Me Party. Even though there was minimal instruction and others were participating, once my awareness focused on the process at hand, it was just me, the paints, and the paper. I lost track of time.

When I finished, feeling satisfied and happy, I stepped back, and the painting's rich colors reflected a veritable horror show. Even though I'd been both contemplative and joyful in the process, the result illustrated inner pain and conflict that I could now look at differently. It was on paper staring back at me. I struggled to not overanalyze and simply let it be.

Gathered round, we shared how the act of painting felt for each of us—an abundance of good—and then Melody asked, "What do you see in your painting? How do you feel when you look at it?"

"A little surprised," I chimed in. "I had fun painting, but I see a shattered shark cage, an electric eel, oozing entrails, and billowing blood of what's left of the poor diver which, in passing, vaguely seemed like seaweed and frilly-tailed fish when I was painting. From a distance, the meaning was suddenly very emotional and complex."

Melody responded, "But you were playful when painting, and then it brought up other emotions for further meditation and fresh painting. You can let the process lead you to more understanding, perhaps of this scene or another."

As the first day of the workshop came to a close, I shared my gratitude with her before glancing excitedly at the richly-colored paints on my paper. The scene reminded me of my childhood and how I hid emotional pain to not upset those who inflicted it as I knew it would only bring more pain to me, either by seeing them suffer or by my suffering their retaliation. These themes often appeared in my personal writing over the years. As I left, I was excited to get to my journal.

Just as the colors and brushstrokes created images in my painting experience, you have assembled words in your journal from your daily life. And as the painting conveyed meaning, the words you have placed on the page now invite you to take a fresh look.

As you did to build your journaling practice, I offer these techniques which served me well. Again, these are not rules, but four flexible suggestions which have helped me make the best of my review process and encouraged more writing to strengthen my journaling practice. Use what feels right for you and let other ideas prompt you to create unique guidelines to enhance your process.

READY TO REVIEW

Journaling encourages the opportunity to be an open book to yourself during the process of writing and then again in review when you permit the words to reflect truth back to you. Your journaled words are a mirror of your humanity and spirit, revealing where you feel complete and connected, where you witness growth and potential, and where you see rising challenges and ideas.

First, give thanks for the written pages of your practice. Breathe in the joy. Feel the triumph of this attained goal. Take a minute to grasp this warmth in your mind, your body, your heart, and your spirit.

Now, take another breath and notice how you feel about your forthcoming review. Are you excited? Nervous? Frightened? If it feels right, take a moment and journal these feelings, even writing questions as prompts to answer later. If insecure, consider contacting a trusted one to determine if now is or is not a good time for your review, as well as to secure support for this process.

You may wonder if you need to review, and that's reasonable. When I first approached review, I was skeptical, primarily since I overcame the difficult work to move beyond my desire to read and evaluate each entry as I grew my practice. So, I again had to build trust that even if the review process wasn't comfortable or didn't seem worthwhile, I would be okay.

Create techniques to start your review, and just like you've adjusted your practice as it has grown, adapt as needed. I print my journal from the computer document, then label passages by embellishing them with a variety of colored highlighters, connecting topics by flagging them with multi-colored, self-stick page markers, and adorning significant lines with doodles, such as hearts for those that touched me, smiley faces for those that made me happy, and frowning faces for those that made me sad. I also use stars next to words and phrases ripe to become writing prompts.

Because my journal remains intact within a computer document, one which can easily be printed again, I have no problem with my notation. However, if notating your journal disrespects the process or taints a personal document you want to keep pristine, don't do it. Use sticky notes for writing remarks, or perhaps number pages and create a list that refers to certain subjects. I knew a journaler who created a simple spreadsheet to index significant dates, topics, comments, and potential prompts. If you want to notate further, make photocopies. Recognize what feels good to you and go for it.

Decide upfront or play it loose within review as to how you interact with new prompts and questions. Basically, I flip through notations after review and make a bulleted list of prompts for later use. Some journalers notate in text or write the newly prompted entry, either at the spot of inspiration or on a fresh page at the end of current writing. This is simple in a computer doc, and for handwritten journals, new loose-leafed pages can be inserted, even into a bound journal.

The review process can feel daunting, but it doesn't have to be a burden if your heart is in it. Clear your mind of opposition and read a little faster, noticing when you slow down and where you linger. Maybe make a note of it.

Remind yourself of the principles you've engaged to complete these personal pages and use them in this new part of the process. Safety afforded you freedom to write your whole truth. Awareness provided a multi-leveled, ever-broadening perspective to witness your outer and inner world. And commitment fueled your journey to understand your spirit and creativity as you grow.

Now, add detachment, so you can review without judgment. Of course, you will reach conclusions in this activity, but recall that if you criticize yourself, you may shut down the process of centered self-reflection, as well as future journaling. Remember your discovery of Never Mind and how it has hindered you? Remember the work you've done—and probably are still doing—to remove these blocks from your consciousness? Don't condemn yourself by fortifying current negativity or fabricating anew. You know you've grown in many ways through written expression, and evaluation is a logical next step. Good results feel imminent, and since you've seen a beam of light, why go back to darkness? You are already practiced for times when you discover and illuminate your personal shadows, plus you know how to write affirmations to shift your thinking and bolster self-worth. Use these tools in review. Also, consider writing an affirmation specifically for detachment within the review process.

Respond during Review

Now, it's time to read.

For my first review many years ago, I approached the process romantically, thinking it would be like sitting in a vault of gold, gemstones, and trophies, my personal treasure of prized thoughts, feelings, actions, and observations in my own words. In reality, it was more like kneeling in a cold mountain stream, sifting through muddy silt to find a nugget that had a vague glimmer. I found a fair amount of my writing to be dull, even excruciatingly tiresome. Never Mind brandished this as evidence that journaling wasted a ton of time, adding to my frustration as I faced many more pages to review.

I recalled how my trust had to grow in the journaling process itself, and I applied the same "do my best" attitude to review. I also remembered having mixed feelings when I began journaling and how I learned to face them through the writing. Next, I reflected on how good it felt to journal these words, and even if mundane, I recognized they fulfilled their purpose in the writing. So, I wrote an affirmation for a positive outcome without being attached to certainties.

> I honor myself and my journal's content in review, grateful that each word has provided a service to my spirit while knowing that some will rise to recognition and linger in an ongoing supportive role.

Finally, I felt willing to try and ready to discover. Grateful for every line, I moved on with keen awareness for words which lifted my spirit and sparked more exploration. I knew illumination came from both the blinding blaze of the sun and the faintest twinkle of the farthest star. I looked for those lights which showed my way in the moment. And I highlighted them on the page.

For you, emotions may appear from discomfort and shame, to joy and delight, to anger and mistrust, to harmony and love. Are they different takes on a broader theme? What needs attention? Creativity? Enhancement? The message may be crystal clear, or you may feel tension or resistance in your thoughts or body as you encounter them through the reading.

The key is to recognize, make note, and reflect upon them. Do you feel content that the story is complete and its emotions are fully revealed and satisfied, or is more journaling part of this process? Are you willing to remain committed, stay safe, and be aware while continuing to write further on the current topic? If so, notate a prompt for more journaling, or you could also write from your previously written words. Whether now or later, do what suits you best in this creative moment.

When needed, inquire in the writing. Explore who, what, when, where, why, and how to illuminate the picture. Be aware of both the quirky and sublime. Ask where you were in the physical, emotional, and mental realms, as well as where you are in the present. Journal your answers to examine puzzling passages and uncover your unique discovery.

If you feel down on yourself for being a grouch or a complainer through your journaling, well, you may have discovered a shift to strive for. You know how grumbling to an inner-circle confidante without making efforts to move forward can wear down or end a relationship? This dynamic can also happen personally, resulting in a loss of self-esteem. Like a recurring bad dream, the energy behind your writing's repeated message can reenact in other nightmarish ways until you finally wake up to create a new reality. Your words signal you to stop and look at this issue. Use as much ink as needed to boldly boil dilemmas down to their essence, and then invoke your intuition and imagination to inspire beneficial feelings and favorable actions in your writing. Encourage every little spirited step forward, and then write about the actions you took and how they turned out. Recognize your personal effort and be grateful for the gift you've given yourself.

Would responding with a pointed affirmation assist you? And if what you create seems false, recognize that it is because, honestly, you don't have it yet. Keep in mind that the feeling encouraging the belief is the predecessor to the desired presence in your life. Understand that the affirmation first sets your awareness on alert for each advance toward the good you seek. When you begin to recognize each one of these and make your choice on whether to take it or not, your affirmation is doing its work. And remember to give thanks for the awareness to re-energize it to bring more possibilities for your reaction. Keep the affirmation alive in mind until you receive what you want.

You may notice you have written passages, or even pages, where you've checked out from your own reality, ignoring personal difficulties. Did you shift into denial, or was this a much-needed breather from annoyances? If so, do you notice inklings of ideas or return to face the issues in later pages? Once noticed and journaled, affirm your awareness to expand energy and grow more positivity in both your writing and life.

Fiona's recognition came through a pesky pattern in her writing. She bemoaned, "I used the same words over and over. I have two advanced degrees. I should know better!"

"So?" I replied. "This isn't a dissertation. Your journal is just for you. Relax and be confident in the process to be honest with yourself. Besides, you might really resonate with specific words. Look at them again and see if they say something particular to you."

Back home, she noticed the word "anyway" started many paragraphs. Underlining and then reviewing each, she found every preceding paragraph illustrated an aspect of the strict boundaries placed on her creativity by her parents. Whenever the topic veered too close to a painful truth, she abruptly wrote "anyway" to transition away from the resentment she never disclosed, hiding it behind a different topic.

Fiona realized the word was an exposed undercover agent of her Never Mind. She understood how it was hustling her to an artificial sense of safety, shoving her distress down so she wouldn't have to face it. In a gutsy move, she made "anyway" a gateway prompt to continue what she blocked from writing. Her pent-up anger emerged, something she had always felt was disrespectful to her parents. However, by taking each paragraph above that keyword and finishing the writing of her innermost thoughts, she owned it, put it in perspective, and then grew strength for nurturing her inner child who couldn't handle those feelings decades before. When with her parents, it wasn't necessary to bring it up. She had journaled through her pain to a place where she had no anger left to express. Fiona became the supportive parent to herself and shared more love with her folks and others too. And now, she pauses when "anyway" opens a new paragraph in her journal, taking it as a reminder to stop and feel if she's fully finished with the previous subject before moving on.

Similar to Fiona noticing a shift in perspective, now and again, the last sentence of a passage stunned me with its truth. Often, I would not recall writing it. In review, I noticed my point of view jumped from first to second person, like "I always struggle with loneliness during times like these. The only way you can move to peace is through the problem." At first, I disavowed this affirmative guidance, denying I had the ability to create it. Then I considered that maybe I had written enough of my complaints and procrastinations to finally wear down Never Mind, clearing space for a greater truth to appear. As in meditation where mind-chatter must slow to open gaps before guidance can be received, I had to write enough about the topic before this intuitive message could break the surface of my consciousness and land on the page.

Notice how other journaled words are light, perhaps amusing. You feel the warmth and playfulness. Realize that this is not only a feeling as you read, but it was also a feeling you had during the writing and likely one you experienced in the incident which inspired it. This feeling rekindles because you saturated your writing with joy some time ago. Isn't that fantastic? Just like negativity, positivity can linger and repeat. And why not prompt yourself to write more on these happy times? Balance always enhances your practice. These significant words are also ideal to feature in your affirmations.

Within the English language, many words have multiple synonyms and slightly different meanings. Play with words which captivate or encourage. Earlier, I mentioned "gratitude" as a simple prompt to get you away from ill will by looking at your life through an empowering lens. Find words which have a positively profound meaning or let them find you. Notice your emotions, remembering the strongest feelings have the most to offer and then see where your writing takes you.

RENEW AFTER REVIEW

You've completed your journal review, so now eat good food, get good rest, and take good care. Would you feel rejuvenated by meditating, participating in another type of artistic expression, or sharing with a trusted one, such as an elder, friend, or counselor? Sometimes knowing these options are at hand is enough to feel strength to move forward. Do what feels suitable for you.

And yes, remember to pay close attention to your daily happenings and nighttime dreams. Begin to mull over if it's time for a revision—a renewed vision—of what you want in both your practice and your life. Ponder in your journal. You are well accomplished in your skills at holding safety, being aware, and exercising commitment. And your creativity will lead as the process calls for adaptation or expansion, both on and off the page.

Whereas many prompts are a quick means to an end as journaled satisfaction comes in one sitting, some prompts encourage repeat usage. Elevate them from a singular occurrence to a weekly or daily activity.

Nowadays, I still freely pour out words in my journal while I also visit recurring prompts, writing on those which are relevant that day. And I commit to each prompt until such a time when my focused writing has increased my awareness, feeling satisfied that growth is on a steady upswing or I have gotten the lesson. At times, I simply want to shift focus. Either way, I move forward, adding new prompts as needed.

For example, I wanted more compassion in my life, so I used the prompt, "Waking with Compassion," placing it after the one encouraging the writing of last night's dreams. This helped me recognize and change my pattern of negative thinking when I woke in the morning, replacing anxiousness with affirmation to start the new day. Through this prompt, I also addressed waking in the dark of night with worries, my most consistent time for floods of fear from Never Mind. This has built a foundation for additional peace, starting from the edges of consciousness into the subconscious, and possibly further down into the depths of the unconscious, all by focusing on how I awaken from sleep. Those patterns of thought are deeply held, but I remain patient, affirming every inch forward without fear of falling back by being compassionate with myself.

"Living with compassion" was added next, chronicling both when I showed compassion or could have shown more to self and others. After addressing this prompt for a month, I noticed that whenever I was in a tough situation, I still reacted from old patterns, but more and more quickly after the fact, I asked myself how I could have chosen and exhibited compassion. Eventually, this came up in the moment of my difficulty and shifted the results.

I also closed my journaling with the prompt "How is my spirit's compassion guiding me today?" to write intention and optimism for the day ahead. Some mornings, this seemed like a to-do list, while on others it felt like a wish list which heartened me to honor my belief that what I think, feel, do, and write attracts what I desire. Later, I notice when guidance appears, then I give thanks and journal about it. Of course, intuition had been there all along, but this encouraged my connection through elevated trust to open my heart. It also allowed me to easily recognize the distractions disguised as guidance from Never Mind.

One morning when scrolling through a website of re-blogged images, commentary, and jokes, I found a pair of questions and jotted them in my journal. "What do I want?" and "What am I afraid of?" struck a chord with me. I typed in my immediate answer: "I am afraid of what I want." Definitely not an affirmation, so I noticed the alluring attraction of these queries as I shared both my desire and the fear which keeps me blocked from receiving it. Next, I added another prompt—"What I tell myself matters"—and went on to affirm a new positive truth rephrasing my answers' written words. Soon, I began to end my practice by scrolling through recently created affirmations, stopping randomly and reading them aloud. This fresh habit lifted my spirit, and I'll use it, maybe adapt it, until a newly revealed prompt inspires me.

In another way, one often more difficult, we relive challenging times illustrated in our journals through review. These present opportunities to strengthen ourselves and reap the benefits of a better life through living and learning as a natural part of being human. Prompting intentional journaling, as well as a closer look at words written, this renewed vision encourages recovery and revival.

I have used my written words and their review to move through the dynamics and emotions of challenging health, collapsing relationship, and devastating grief. My journal is the lamp shining its light on dark personal times, so I can find my way to a more stable place. When I reach a standstill on something I have explored in my journal, I use the review process to guide me to understand and clarify issues, so I can confer with a trusted one.

My divorce was such a time which included weekly sessions with a therapist. In true Virgo fashion, the process toward each meeting began with a review of my recent journal entries and notation of relevant passages. Next, I made an outline for the appointment, so a number of pages concentrated into talking points and questions with examples from my writing. Though I usually summarized for spoken sharing, I sometimes read passages verbatim within the oath-bound safety of my therapist's office. However, I never gave my writing to the therapist to read, much less to file away. From each interaction, I wrote more and then reviewed my subsequent journaling before another appointment to keep me in check and on course for next steps. My writing grounded me to speak, helped make the best use of each 50-minute session, plus provided a safe place to return for further exploration. Also, when needed, I employed the notes for gaining perspective from other trusted ones.

Some of the subjects I journal are processing thoughts and feelings that I want to share with others, but I am not ready as they are too personal or painful. I respect my feelings and growth, plus I also respect the people in my life too much to dump on them, whether they are sought for support or the one involved. Expelling this raw stuff through writing is healthier for everyone, and journaling often brings the understanding and courage which can lead to an appropriate way to share.

I find it difficult to be fully honest with certain people, whether making an amends for my behavior or voicing my experience of their harms. To improve these skills, I start with myself, exploring emotions and beliefs in my journal. Then, when I open up to others, I trust myself to speak from my abbreviated notes. This reminds me that I've considered the situation and relationship important enough to be prepared, something respectful to us both. I feel clear in discussion while also being present to the other person's thoughts.

If having a conversation feels unhealthy, even risky, you may consider mediation with therapeutic or legal counsel. With notes in hand, I have participated in this with someone when our rationality had been tainted with anger, and this process moved us to resolution. If interaction feels dangerous, don't put yourself in that position. Use your reflection from your journal as a starting point to work toward personal closure and possibly preparation to speak to a trusted one.

Writing a letter is also an appropriate and effective way to share. Know this is using the process of journaling—a commitment to write honestly for your eyes only—and moving to create a product, one meant for a specific, intended audience. You are not directly sharing your journaled words but allowing them to be a springboard to the words you will share after reviewing and revising to your comfort level.

I practiced using my process for product to a simpler end by inscribing cards for birthdays, weddings, and celebrations. From journaling freely, I then focused on this specific person and time, re-reading and modifying the words before handwriting a card or letter with my crafted message. And I let go of who else may read it, knowing I can't control what will happen to my written words once delivered. In fact, if there's something I don't feel comfortable to include in the case that it's read by someone other than the intended receiver, I leave it out to feel confident in the message I am extending.

Whereas the image and messaging of cards are wonderful, especially on occasions when words are difficult to come by, I pushed myself to write from my heart on notes of condolence. From experience in my journal, writing copiously on Mom's illness and decline, I fostered familiarity in accessing those emotions. So, when I learned of a friend who experienced the passing of a person, a pet, or a relationship, among other losses, I journaled my feelings before writing those of sympathy and comfort to share. This not only helped me process my feelings of the loss, but it afforded a personal statement to those special to me who were left behind.

When a dear friend with Alzheimer's went into memory care, I researched about writing for those with memory issues. I journaled my feelings and memories, boiling them down to small vignettes that could be read repeatedly. I paired each with an appropriate card and often glued a photo of us inside for a visual spark. The journaling and its words brought tears and helped ground me in the truth of the situation. It also felt like the best gift I could give her at this stage in her life.

In a very different circumstance, I began with a journaling process to communicate with someone who was toxic. Conversations rarely produced understanding, prohibiting mutual trust and growth. Through much reflection in my journal and with trusted ones, I recognized that I had been gaslighted—intentionally lied to and manipulated—left questioning what I knew and unable to tell the difference between my suspicion and my intuition. Clearly, the relationship had moved from being enjoyable to being intriguing to being stressful to being unsafe. In my efforts to reclaim my spirit, I wrote a very long letter, conferred with my therapist, finalized intended goals, revised, then shared the letter with close friends. I also journaled about the emotions I felt through the process and, when needed, received assistance. After further revision, the brief letter was complete, including gratitude for good times, acknowledging recent changes without blame, then stating my choice to sever ties. I felt good about my honesty and my boundaries. Still, as strange as it may seem, it took some time to convince myself to send it. I journaled that fear and other feelings too. Once mailed, I wrote my various reactions, some quite surprising. And after many quiet months, I accepted my gratitude for the resolution alongside the need for more processing. I discovered that, like experiencing a death, I had to grieve. Loss never disappears; it simply settles over time into a new reality of life. Along with the steps in this process, journaling allowed me to forgive the issues and recover the light. And I trusted that as time moved on, my journal would be amongst the trusted ones who continued to support me.

If the person with whom you desire resolution is deceased, you can write to them, even share the letter and speak with a trusted one, maybe someone who also knew them. Ask if they are willing to be present and perhaps participate in conversation to help you reach a satisfactory conclusion. Then, return to the page to journal toward closure.

Remember, as we experience how our journal writing illustrates our personal stories, often we assert our narrative as our identity. Yet, we are so much more than our story. We have so much potential and possibility. Our story is just who we *think* we are, while in reality, it's just the place *where* we are. We always have the option for renewal, to make new choices and create a better life.

This goes for your journaling too. What more do you want from your practice? How can you encourage yourself and grow as a journaler? And if you haven't yet identified it, make it a prompt—perhaps one visited often—looking at what thoughts, feelings, actions, and intuitions illuminate your unique writing spirit.

Keep Writing

So, now what? Whether you feel like you've grown in your practice or not, your next steps may honestly be what you've done before. And if you feel that way, you're right! Whether you feel stalled, stumped, or pumped up, remember the honest solution is "journal about that."

For my practice, I still follow the suggestions—not rules—mentioned in chapter two, but I flex them a little. Every morning, I begin journaling anew as I, myself, am renewed too! And I do it again the next day…

I don't review because I pay attention to myself in the moment, feeling the balance in my writing. When I do review, it's rarely extensive or seldom more than once a month. And I am also not inclined to edit. I learned when I wrote by hand that editing was not only disruptive to flow, but messy on the page. I could easily remedy this in my computer doc, but I don't because, even though the messiness disappears, it will show in the mental-emotional scramble of my process. Additionally, I edit writing in my business most days each week, so not editing in my journal is a freedom I savor and celebrate. For all journal writers, editing is not important in this process.

Just like any day, journal fresh in your present perspective. Lean into knowing you are created of creativity to be creative, and then relax and record the words which come to you.

Rely on the tried-and-true tools which serve you—particularly if Never Mind spouts opposition—and move forward because moving forward is building your practice. Trust your writing will provide answers *in* the writing for you to experience them both now and in review.

Build on your momentum. What new approaches work for you? Revisit ideas found in your review, even some from earlier in the book, and stay open to your creative contributions.

Declare your truth with heartfelt affirmations and write new ones. Write on the prompts you found, maybe try some recurring prompts, and keep your list active.

Engage in safety to journal freely. When conclusions come, express what feels right and call out what doesn't, including your own biases and Never Mind's harsh judgments. Stand tall in your safety and be courageously vulnerable.

Be aware of all that's inside your consciousness and what's arising from your subconscious, as well as all that you attract around you. Observe and be in the moment. Reflect in your journal and then again, whenever you're ready, in your next review.

Remain committed, or maybe light a candle and have a re-commitment ceremony in writing to expand this feeling. I have done this, and the candle's flame celebrated a continued path forward in its beautiful light. Journal a little deeper and broader, asking questions and letting answers come to you.

Look at other qualities that may be key to your practice. Just as I mentioned adding detachment to your review, what feels good to employ in your journaling? Kindness? Wisdom? Integrity? Love? I bet you know...

And exercise all of this wrapped in the warmth of gratitude for your practice, your life, and your writing spirit.

Walking into Melody's studio the next day, my crinkled painting hung on the easel. I looked at the mangled shark cage, and it didn't feel horrible. I busted that memory open when I painted, releasing remorse from years before, plus I had journaled about a concealed wound, both after yesterday's workshop and before the one this morning.

Unpinning the painting, readying for a new piece of paper, I remembered awakening with a vision. I sheepishly asked Melody, "Is it okay if I paint from a dream I had last night?" I knew this wasn't encouraged as the process was simply to let paint, paper, and brushes lead, but the dream's mystical cat kept purring as it tickled my imagination.

Melody's face lit up. "Let it be a starting point."

I smiled, feeling an openhearted playfulness—That one!—silently grabbing a brush and swiftly dipping it into the sunshine yellow tempera. I painted the tail of the cat, then the body outline and head, then kept painting, following the pull of the colors and strokes of the brushes as new patterns emerged, delightfully surprising me like images in a dream.

As I kept my attention on the brush, the color, and the paper, I recognized a profound clarity that I knew from my journaling practice. I knew this peaceful feeling when I focused on the lines of copy, the sentences, the phrases...then adding another and another, moving ahead a word at a time. These words blended to illuminate truth, engage my spirit, and encourage me onward to, once again, answer the call of my journal's empty-page prompting. And I knew that someday I might again reflect in review of this magical message as I returned to the movement and hues of the moment.

11

Reflection

AFFIRMING A JOURNALER'S CONSCIOUSNESS

Use affirmations, one or all, adapting as desired.

My journal is an open book to myself as I write, and then again as I review when my words reflect truth back to me.

I am grateful for having journaled these words, and even if mundane to read, their purpose was served in the writing.

I develop methods for my journal's review, extending the honor and respect I have for my writing into new realms.

Like life, journal writing and its reading are an ongoing process of honesty, discovery, and growth for my spirit.
I feel free.

Alongside principles of safety, awareness, and commitment, I add detachment to review without judgment, encouraging self-reflection and enhancing my journaling practice.

I now see that expelling raw emotions in my journal is healthy for me and others, plus this writing lights the path to appropriate sharing away from the page.

When I find unsettled or intriguing matters in my journal, I create writing prompts, then dialogue with them on paper.

My written words offer the chance to look at myself, to reflect and revise, to create a new vision of a life more desired.

I cheer every word written and every word reviewed, as well as every word these acts have inspired for further journaling.

I write from prompts in my journal, and some encourage repeat usage, so I elevate these to an ongoing activity.

My journal is a personal process, not a product to share.

I wrap myself in the nourishing warmth of gratitude for my life, my journaling practice, and my writing spirit.

Write an affirmation about utilizing reflection.

- o Begin with either "I am…" or "I…" followed by an action verb in present tense, such as fortify, tickle, or notate.
- o Complete with heartfelt words to lift your spirit and motivate your growth.

11

Reflection

PROMPTING A JOURNALER'S PRACTICE

Choose a word or phrase,
and then journal what comes up.

o   Hesitant fake-smile

o   Sanctum

Complete the sentence and write more.

o   "I could have shown more compassion to self and others when..."

Create your own prompt and journal from it.

o

12

Writing Spirit

I trust myself
as I extend
my practice,
journaling to
fresh facets of
my writing spirit.

A Celebration of Life

"There's a cake on my head," he proclaimed, waking just as suddenly as he had fallen asleep moments ago.

Yellowed with jaundice, Emmett was in intensive care with so many wires attached and tubes inserted that overhearing the attending physician and nurse pondering where to put a port for a blood transfusion was more than I could handle. And now this.

"Em, you don't have a cake on your head," I said in an attempt at clarity and compassion.

"You don't know," he snapped.

A nurse-friend had instructed me to help him stay present if he became delusional. Just minutes before, he asked about the treasure map on his bed. I thought this might have something to do with his love of ancient Egypt, but I couldn't consider it. So, I affirmed his imagination while clinging to my fading hope that he was just spinning a story and not really spinning away from me. I asked him to be real, so all of us—loved ones and caring staff—could help him. He needed to be present. We all did.

"No, I don't know," I said while internally shouting back my own tears and fears. "I just don't see a cake on your head."

"There are more in the closet."

I took a step back and looked around the room, even past the curtain to an empty bed, then, just to make sure, to the corners where I had not given much attention. Briefly pausing to glance out the slim, solitary window at the Atlanta skyline, I took a deep breath before returning my gaze to him.

"Em, there isn't a closet."

"Yes, there is."

"Buddy, look around. You're in the ICU at Grady. Trust me, there isn't a closet in this room."

He turned away and so did I, both frustrated, perhaps for different reasons. When we reconnected, his eyes pleaded as he requested help swinging his legs off the bed so he could more easily pee. As I listened to him, the nurse on the other side of the bed looked at me and shook her head. I calmly explained I couldn't do that for him, then whispered, "I'm sorry." I truly was.

Em was like a brother to me, always protective while encouraging me to live life to its fullest. Through the years, his intelligence, creativity, wit, and depth of perceptions comingled with mine for fascinating conversations, veering from playful to philosophical to emotional. And even when we disagreed, we usually found our way back to laughter. Now, more than I ever had in our lifelong relationship, I ached to be his support, but I truly felt helpless as his light dimmed.

After a few more minutes by his bedside as he drifted in and out of sleep while the staff continued their hushed debate, he opened his tired eyes and looked into mine. I gently cradled his swollen hand, then leaned over, kissing him on the forehead. Our faces close together, I told him I loved him, and he looked at me and said, "I love you too."

In the waiting room, I talked with his parents who, since my time rooming with Emmett in college, were family to me. I shared of my leaving first thing tomorrow for a quick getaway to Las Vegas planned months ago. I had journaled earlier that morning about choices, about risks in life and love, and about how some blended sweet joy with sour dread. After seeing him, my anxiety boiled over.

His mother, my Mama Linda, shared concern alongside her belief that he would be fine. "You need this, and besides, we both know he would want you to go."

Being a slot machine bandit, she lightened the mood by giving me hints on how to win, tips like looking for the machine that glowed pink as it readied to pay off. She did everything but whisk me to the airport as she soothed my worries, promised me I'd hear of any changes, and encouraged me to take care of myself. Still, I knew leaving for Vegas was a huge gamble.

Eighteen hours later, the garish colors of the desert city beckoned from thousands of feet below. Descending into turbulence, I tensed up as the plane swayed and dipped all the way to touching down. Rushing to baggage claim, I met my friend B.J. for my virgin Vegas tour. After a day of catching up, settling in her timeshare, and surveying the surreal town, I slept hard, readying for the long weekend.

At 5 a.m., my ringing cellphone catapulted me conscious. I stood, pitifully grasping to the hope that this was just a fear dream.

Answering, I heard one of Em's friends crying on the other end. "He's gone."

Looking out the sliding glass door at the pool and its romantically-lit palm trees blowing wildly in the wind, I knew I had lost my closest friend. And as abruptly as it came, the call ended.

Engulfed in guilt and grief, I felt utterly helpless as I cried alone in that dark hotel room all the way across America. I pulled my pad and pen from the suitcase, hearing repeated invitations to the page, but I had no strength to answer. All I could do was be present and eke out some whispered splinters of affirmations between sobs and memories.

At daybreak, Dora, Emmett's sister, called, firm in her reassurance for me to stay, that the funeral would not be held until I returned. "He'd want you to enjoy yourself," she said, knowing neither of us could fathom that happening.

As I searched for what to say, she cried and admitted, "I never believed he would die."

"I didn't either," I said, choking up. "He'd been close before and always bounced back."

When the sun intensified, B.J. emerged from her room and joined me, supporting me in my sorrow.

I functioned on autopilot for the next few days, and I wasn't journaling. Not that I wouldn't have felt lost at home, but I didn't bring my laptop, and having to write in long hand became an easy excuse to avoid it altogether. I had no room for more regret as I gave myself permission to be away from the page, knowing I would journal soon enough.

I didn't feel connected to my body in the natural radiance of Red Rock Canyon, at the man-made marvel of Hoover Dam, or amidst the flamboyant fanfare of the Vegas strip. I thought of Emmett everywhere, particularly in the Egyptian-themed, pyramid-shaped Luxor Hotel. Strolling through on my own, I became disoriented as I took countless double takes, glimpsing his face on one person after another after another.

The morning after my return, I found the newspaper obituary online, printed it, then left it on my desk in the light of my infallible floor lamp so the words could verify this new reality. On my computer, I set a slide show of vacation pictures of Em and I in Mexico Beach on Florida's panhandle. Then I opened my journal document, placed my fingers on the home keys, and started with the words at the front of a crowded queue. I wrote and wrote, crying as my emotional dam burst, and all the thoughts, feelings, and memories pushed their way out. Some birthed a tender phrase while the juggernaut of others powered an unstoppable paragraph over multiple pages. I barely took time to blow my nose with one hand while the other held steady in its home-key position, preparing for the next torrent of expression.

After an hour, I got up for a large glass of water, and then washed my face and cleaned my tear-speckled glasses, avoiding a glance in the bathroom mirror before returning for more. Later, I took the laptop to bed, sitting up to use my outstretched legs as a desk, a box of tissues at the ready. I poured out my anguish, my regrets, my guilt, and my fears amongst scattered thoughts like how we met in first grade but soon ended up on different sides of the county and didn't share a school again until we happened into the same dorm elevator shortly after arrival at the University of Georgia. I flashed back to living off campus with him during my last year of college, discovering his odd sleep schedule and how hypnotic he seemed when he burned things in the fireplace. I wrote how he helped inspire my true voice, and I cried for the loss of his inspiration. Then I pondered if it really was gone, and in baby steps, I began to connect with a glimmer of this possibility.

At the traditional funeral with an organist playing hymns and ministers doing their sincere best to describe a man they never met, my grief left me vulnerable to the doubt and blame that were in full force.

I should have been with him. Why was I so stupid, so selfish?

Even with the answers in my heart, the processing in my journal, and the soul searching before the trip, there was neither a crystal ball to look into for what I should have done nor a clock to turn back time. I knew I had made the best decision I could have. Maybe I wasn't meant to be with him, but I would never know. And now I had to live with it.

While stuffing my sorrow from a plate piled high with helpings of every chocolate dessert at the reception, Em's adult niece, Lindy, came over. She shared that, to help with her grief, she researched Egyptology, a tip of the iceberg of his lifelong fascination. As she spoke, memories appeared, like when he shaved his eyebrows to mourn his cat's passing, and his interjecting the alignment of the pyramids into any topic. As Lindy continued, I flashed back to my otherworldly visions of him in the Luxor, amidst the eerily-lit surroundings, remembering how time seemed warped. Then I snapped back to the moment as she told me of her discovery that the first step for bodies entering the mummification process was to have a loaf of unleavened bread placed on their head.

So, Emmett did have a cake on his head. He knew...and I really didn't.

I smiled at this realization, this gift, and mercifully forgave myself a little.

Lindy asked if I would like to join Emmett's family and friends in planning a celebration of life. I instantly agreed, offering to pull together the program and facilitate, then felt the fear in my body and heard the overwrought worries from Never Mind.

Can you live with yourself if you make another huge mistake? Can you get centered enough to organize, much less speak in front of everyone? You are not capable to handle this while you are grieving. What if you muck this up?

Clearly, I knew this mission would bring up my doubts. Even with experience in event facilitation and public speaking, there would be a lot of conflicting emotions on top of all the ones already present. Still, in my thoughts, I affirmed:

> I am safe. Though I will do my best, I may fail, and that's okay. I am surrounded by loved ones, and I want to be true to my spirit, just like I did with Emmett. I am ready, and with all my heart, I want to do this.

With purpose, I immediately began ramping up my journaling about Emmett. I wrote in my usual process, focusing on Em and me without formulating a plan for what I would share at the celebration. I trusted myself to be authentic, creatively expressing while grieving. I affirmed these truths to quiet Never Mind, fully allowing the presence of intuition and insight. Even with a mere month before the event, my goal was simple: support my spirit and keep journaling.

I wrote page after page, topics taking flight, laughing and crying at will. I flew with them, surrendering to the streaming flow of consciousness to frolic in the bountiful memories rising from my subconscious. The catharsis was wonderful, and though the pain wasn't alleviated—not that I expected that—I felt a newfound balance. Instead of spiraling downward, my creativity used the motion as a catalyst to fly, twist, and loop-de-loop, thus energizing the process.

The ceremony's plans moved forward, the date approached, and soon it was time for me to review my journal, finding passages to steer toward organization to speak to his family and community. I readied by shifting my mind from process to product, looking for excerpts which felt alive in story and emotion while remaining committed to the safety and enjoyment for both the audience and me. As I reviewed, I responded in writing, revising rough edges and removing the too-personal portions. I also took breaks to renew my spirit and remain grounded in the task by journaling how I felt in the moment.

I had never spoken my spirit's truth to such a group with diverse beliefs. From compassionate integrity, I had to come out as my unique self to fully express my sensitivity through vulnerability, to develop trust with the attendees, and to engage for authentic interaction. I considered the attendees of various ages and belief systems—some religious, some spiritual, some not—most I didn't know well, but who, like me, knew Emmett. I wanted to be mindful and honor everyone's beliefs. From that intention, I received intuitive guidance for words which would resonate and touch hearts. And I wrote them down.

On a scorching spring day in May 2011, we readied the memorial's displays, food, and flowers at the event facility, a beautiful Victorian home and garden. I created a writing station for guests in a shaded gazebo, and then I moved into the sunlight to a pedestaled tin bucket, originally meant for icing drinks. I covered the bottom with several inches of sand, lit a large jar candle, and placed it in the center. I arranged flowers, herbs, and ferns around the base of this vessel where written expressions would be set aflame for release. Overcome by heat and emotion, sweat poured off my bald head in the place of the tears I suppressed.

Alone in the bride's quarters, a small, secluded apartment in the rear of the facility, I hung my suit on the back of the door and stripped to my skivvies while fanning myself with the ceremony outline and story notes. In the quiet, Never Mind took advantage of the opportunity.

It's not too late to back out.

I looked at my reddened face in the mirror and rolled my eyes.

Rehearse the lines again. This is important, and there's only one chance.

I stopped fanning and looked at the words, but they blurred in my overheated head. This signaled that, at this point, the notes were much better used as a fan. I needed to sit, center, and feel peaceful before dressing and leaving this safe space. Never Mind continued to direct, but I had become more adept at focusing on the positive, hearing intuition over its interruptions, affirmations over its anxieties. I knew why I was here. Even alone, I felt a sense of belonging. So, I sat with my heart, feeling honored for the gift I was to share, and like my pages of notes working their magic by cooling me, I again affirmed I would do my best. And just as Emmett had been a trusted one for me, now was a fine time to trust myself.

While Em's favorite songs filled the space, I mingled amongst the fifty in attendance. There was as much laughter as tears, often happening simultaneously. As the music faded, I watched from the front as everyone took a seat, then I opened the ceremony.

"In each moment as we continue to learn to live with our loss, it is healing to recall our memories, feel gratitude for them, and share in loving community. Every life is made up of millions of moments and, hence, millions of memories relating to hundreds of thousands of stories which connect to many, many other hearts and souls. Today, we celebrate the life of Emmett, a man we loved to share our lives with, a man who left us with many memories, all with stories attached. Often, they were vivid and quite colorful. I imagine you are connecting to them right now."

I then shared a light, amusing story that demonstrated Em's rarely seen vulnerability through his illogical fear of zombies after a college viewing of the film *Night of the Living Dead*. Over the next hour, others shared stories, both written and off-the-cuff, all lovingly received. Finally, I read a piece about the writing station and the burning bowl.

"Smoke was transformative to Emmett. Along with his ever-present cigarettes, he also loved candles and fireplaces. I first saw him playing in a fireplace in the apartment we shared during senior year at college in 1982. Most of the time, he wasn't building a fire in a traditional sense. Sometimes, he made things just to burn them. Other times, he would be finished with something, like an art project that didn't work out or one he'd looked at long enough, and he would set it on fire. He would burn paper, and for all I know, the pages were covered with things he wanted to release, perhaps to open space to make room for the new.

"Some 25 years later on New Year's Eve of 2007, we got together in his home for a night of making art. We told stories, laughed, kvetched, and created, cackling for hours. Then I shared some letters and photos from college and through our twenties which we were both embarrassed and tickled about, all things that, in retrospect, felt immature but showed growth. Then he pulled out a round aluminum pan to use as a burning bowl. It was filled with mounds of herbs, like basil, sage, and one he acknowledged as my favorite, rosemary. I'd come prepared with things of my own that I wanted to release from a tumultuous year filled with vivid heartache and self-awareness. Emmett was ready too."

My voice cracked as tears rose, so intuition nudged me to pause and breathe.

"We burned letters, greeting cards, and pictures, then we turned our attention to the statements of gratitude we had written earlier that evening, then the wishes that we had for moving forward: wishes for ourselves, wishes for each other, for our families, our friends, and our world. Following our ritual, I felt incredibly light, unburdened, open to magnificent possibility for the year to come, one that would turn out to be our most connected, one full of magical times in Mexico Beach, and one with long, vibrant conversations on the phone or wherever we were.

"So, in the spirit of that burning bowl, those of us who organized this celebration pass that energy to you as a heartfelt invitation. In the gazebo, there are paper and pens for you to express about him and to him. There's a container with a flame in the adjoining garden. Fire is cleansing to life as messages, wishes, prayers, troubles, gratitudes, ideas, declarations, apologies, questions, thoughts, and goodbyes are expressed by writing stories, sentences, phrases, lists, even hieroglyphics, in whatever way you feel guided, and then burned for release. This ritual of letting go honors Emmett, honors you, and honors us all."

I glanced around the gathering and could see the wheels turning. Sniffing back tears, I asked everyone to close their eyes and join me in silence. Seeing the serenity on their faces, I recognized that even with differing beliefs, at heart, we were truly one. We all want to give and receive love, and we all want to be happy. Here, we came mourning death but rose together by celebrating life: Emmett's life and the life in all of us now.

After closing my eyes and taking five deep breaths in the tranquility of the room, I quietly said, "We are blessed to have had Emmett in our lives. We are blessed to have memories of those moments. We are blessed to have new memories of new moments gathered today. Though his life with us is a memory, our shared love with Emmett is still alive this moment and forevermore. We are truly blessed. And so it is. Amen."

I hugged each family member and many friends before joining everyone outside under a tent to relax, eat, and chat. I noticed the pilgrimages to the gazebo for writing as well as the smoke rising from the garden. Most everyone participated, and from the comments I received, they appreciated it and felt a little lighter.

Later, I walked the path to the Gazebo and wrote something on the spot to add to those I had written through the weeks for this ritual. I joined the bright sun at the bowl, now littered with ashes, as I affirmed, lit paper with the flame, and watched it go up in smoke.

As I finished, Dora joined me and, like a magician, whipped sheet after folded sheet of pre-written, yellow legal pages from her tiny, tropical-print purse. As she set one on fire, I lit a stem of rosemary and played in the flames like Em used to, sharing that I had plans for these ashes.

Lighting the edge of another sheet, she asked, "What plans?"

"Well, the story I told about the New Year's Eve burning bowl with Emmett wasn't complete." I explained when he and I went to Mexico Beach that spring and visited a secluded stretch of sand under an eagle's nest, he handed me a baggie with the ashes from our ritual. "He told me, 'You have more to let go. This might help. Give them to the sea.' And I did."

Dora and I both blotted tears and perspiration from our faces.

"So, I'm going back to that beach and give these ashes to the sea too."

After cooling down with some iced tea, alternately drinking from the glass and rolling it on my forehead, I hit the buffet again then sat next to Mama Linda.

"You know," she said, "you were number one on his Las Vegas List."

"I remember him saying that," I said, eating another stuffed mushroom. "Please remind me, what was that list for?"

She leaned over, and her expression showed me again where Emmett got the twinkle in his eye and the mischief in his grin. "That was his written list of who to call to spring him from jail if he were ever in Vegas and got busted."

I beamed as I realized the depth of trust he had in me, then I began to wonder why he chose Vegas as where he would most likely get caught...and for doing what? Impish thoughts lifted the corners of my mouth.

She continued. "I was on the list but never higher than four or five. Fell below ten a couple of times, probably when he was mad at me. Dora usually ranked above me, but you," she paused, "you were always at the top."

I smiled solemnly. Maybe his written list *was* prophetic, that there was some reason why I was in Vegas when he passed. Maybe he really was in the mystical pyramid showing up in the faces of everyone around me, giving me an arresting, trippy way to see him off. Or maybe, like a metaphor in a dream, I was literally "the one he chose to face" in the dizzying succession of his crossing-over farewell performance.

But maybe it was his special gift to show me that death is an interlude, just a blip of turning one page to the next in the writing of this never-ending life story. So, maybe I wasn't in Vegas for him at all, that my being there—sober and in a pyramid, no less—was his final ruse to trick me into something I never would have accepted if I had the chance to overthink it. Maybe being on top of his list was not for me to set him free, but for him to show me how to emancipate myself, opening my spirit to a freedom I had never known. So, even in creative silence, Emmett got his last word, but the gift…the gift was all mine.

Each moment of life has a message which may not be recognized when living it, when remembered, or when reviewed in a journal. But, perhaps in a new moment, that earlier experience and its meaning are the lamp that light the significance in such a way to capture its beauty before it slips away like a dream.

Four years and thousands of journaled words later, I made it to the secluded shore near Mexico Beach with my only plan to fulfill my goal and be present. Loaded with the ashes and a bottle of water in my tote, I headed down the beach, stepping over or going under trees felled by the erosive ocean. I walked to where the eagle's nest used to be, but there was no sign of it in the few remaining pines. This habitat had changed, but I knew I was in the right place.

All alone, I planted my tote on a root ball of a downed palm and mounted the trunk as if it were a horse, pulling out the large baggie of burning bowl cinders. As I shared thanks aloud for those who had written, I dumped the contents on the sand below my dangling feet, surprised by some large paper fragments with indiscernible scribblings amongst the rubble. Surprisingly, the sea seized them in an urgent lunge and swift retreat. From thought to emotion to writing to smoke to ash to sea, all swept away.

I repacked the big baggie to take it away for disposal, then I pulled out a smaller baggie. I held it gently, caressing it in my curled fingers as I pondered a more gracious way to set it free. I stopped thinking and simply listened, first at the waves, then for creative guidance.

In my thoughts, I heard Emmett whisper, "Don't think. Have fun!"

I felt the urge to get off the tree trunk, and when I did, a wave splashed up my side all the way to my chest. Although sealed in plastic, I instinctively held the baggie high above my head and kept it there as I determinedly marched through the brush that grabbed at my bare legs.

Not far away on a clear, intimate spot of beach, I stopped. I dismissed more ideas of plans and didn't linger on the nagging insistence of ceremony, of implied importance encumbering the heart of the matter. As the water gently rolled up to my ankles and then away, I felt my feet sinking into the sand, a movement that felt grounding. My breathing fell in synch with the waves as the words of my affirmations flowed, the water washing ashore, softly sweeping to my right, just enough to subtly stroke all it touched. As I relaxed, the waves subsided. I opened the baggie, and, for the first time, I looked inside at Emmett's cremains.

I uttered a rambling, honest affirmation of gratitude for Emmett in my life and for Dora's gift I enfolded in my fingers, closing with thanks for life in this moment.

I began to quietly cry, realizing that just as I had been told by Em years before on this very spot, I still had more to let go of. The rhythmic sea was ready to oblige.

When I awkwardly started to pour his ashes in my hand, a gust of wind surprised me. I guarded the bag, not wanting the ashes to blow backwards, and right then, I knew I needed to reach inside.

What the—?!

Never Mind screamed fear, so I quickly replaced it with trust. I put my hand in the baggie, and upon contact, I recognized why I felt compelled to do it that way. I had to touch Em one last time.

A mixture of powdery dust and bone fragments stuck to my damp fingers. I squatted as a wave flowed past my feet, and I put my closed fist to the sand as the sea retreated. The trail of color escaping my tight grasp astounded me. The gray ashes streaked a purple-red, and as I opened my hand, the pieces of bone blended with battered bark, seashell shards, and other evidence of lived life reclaimed by nature.

I pulled another handful and another, letting each slip through my fingers into the wave's withdrawal, tenderly letting him go.

With little left, I corralled the final wet clumps in my palm, realizing this would be the last time I would hold my friend.

I tightened my fist as the water rushed in, tears exploding like a summer pop-up storm, overwhelming my eyes and sinuses. And just as quickly, that burst had passed, the emotion depleted, and I fanned my fingers wide in surrender. The purple streak was the most magnificent as it washed, eddied, and faded.

The sun heated my body, the sea washed my feet, and the breeze floated my spirit. Along with losing Em, I had been shaken by many hardships and losses over the past few years, but I was aware that I now viewed life as a cycle with each moment offering a new beginning, even the one immediately upon death. Sure, I had grieving to do, but I also had life to live, and the two often occurred simultaneously. I knew my friendship with Em would never die as love is immortal, and I felt its very presence.

After driving to my rental, I was calm yet excited to journal. I took out a pad and pen with the intention to journal for my spirit, writing in long hand. Glancing at the sunset on the gulf's horizon, I intuitively felt that there would come a time to share this awareness with others, and that feeling eased in and out of my consciousness like a lone ripple at low tide.

The written words which circled these events—my journal pages; the 30-year-old college letters Em and I wrote to one another, then saved to ultimately share again and release together; numerous affirmations; an obit by a small-town journalist; more journal entries; the ceremony notes on the stories of the zombies, the burning bowl, and all the rest revised to speak aloud; the attendees' expressions written and set free by fire; whatever whomever wrote afterwards; the oft-revised versions of Emmett's Las Vegas List; line after line I journaled about the Celebration of Life and my beach ritual; even this chapter I wrote to share—all writing connected writers to life past, present, and future. Our writing, even when kept private, connects us to ourselves, each other, and our spirits.

Just as Emmett enjoyed the freedom found in burning things, I enjoy writing's release. Like he created smoke and watched it swirl, dance, and dissipate, my words delight me as I write, fueling me forward, whatever the tone or message. And I knew that day when I released my dear friend to the waves that I, too, have a Las Vegas List. I have many trusted ones who, through their spirit, remain ready to lift me if I am in need. But when I journal and allow Never Mind to arrest my affirmations, my actions, and my writing, locking me up in the jail of my own fears, I trust the enduring source in my List's number one spot: Creativity. And instantly with this inside call, my writing spirit is free again to live, to love, and to celebrate all aspects of life in my journal.

Now, with love and light, I affirm this truth from my writing spirit to your writing spirit:

> I am a luminary, creativity individualized, an
> essential element for expression in this world.
> Created of creativity to be creative, I am a lamp
> for the light. My spirit resides ready to write in
> my journal.

> As pen moves or fingers fly, I discover inspiration
> by writing for my eyes only. Either through
> a prompt or in the moment's fertile flow of
> thoughts to words, my journaling enlivens
> my spirit and my life with others.

> I supply safety, providing permission, intention,
> and gratitude for good outcomes in and through
> my journaling practice.

> I continually stretch and strengthen my
> journaler's consciousness, utilizing my keen
> senses, thoughts, feelings, and intuition to
> write with full awareness.

> My commitment to passion and freedom stays
> steadfast in my journaling practice. I emancipate
> myself in writing and in life.

Through mindfulness and intuition, I detect
perfection, procrastination, and all fears brought
forth by Never Mind. Then, I write the opposite
of their messages in focused affirmations,
centered on the positive to maintain momentum
in creating a new belief to live by.

My vulnerability is a superpower, uniting my
inner child and outer adult for heightened
perspective and heroic imagination, piling my
plate high with magnificent possibility.

I dream in my waking life and live in my
dreamtime, raising the natural connection
between conscious and subconscious mind
to enhance my journaling.

My life is made up of millions of moments and,
hence, millions of memories. I illuminate all of
who I am in my written words, and I reflect upon
them through periodic review to energize
my practice and deepen my spirit.

I select treasures I have unearthed in writing and
reviewing my journal, sharing them with trusted
ones and my community, either through spoken
word or the example of my authentic being.

In this world, all I have promised is the present moment and the choice of how I live it. I embrace change, empower growth, and choose love. All is good.

Journaling is a celebration of life. Now, in gratitude, I turn to a fresh page in my journal and write. And so it is, the truth of living my writing spirit.

ACKNOWLEDGMENTS

Writing Spirit is bound with the strength, guidance, and love from many generous spirits. Happy tears pooled in my eyes as I reminisced on these trusted ones who have reviewed, notated, listened, reflected, and participated with abundant affection and creativity. All of you have been a vital part of my growth through the years of this book's process to publication.

To Randall Cumbaa, thanks for reading an early version and then sticking with me. From your caring demeanor and sharp vision, you shared both acclaim and questions for my work ahead. You continued to check in on my progress, always willing to lend an ear or a kind word. And when I reached another plateau with the manuscript, you revisited it, giving feedback on my specific challenges. Randall, I am so grateful for your patience in motivating my perseverance throughout this writing journey.

To Jessie Hayden, you felt the passion in my words when I spoke of my journaling practice many years before I ever considered writing a book. I'm grateful that, in 2003, your inspired suggestion and gentle nudge to create and facilitate a journaling class led to my first teaching experience and eventually my coaching business. Years later, you reviewed my book, delivering encouragement from your academic background and compassionate heart. Thank you, Jessie, for gifting me with significant moments that defined my path.

To Elizabeth Ives, we have been friends for over half our lifetimes, beginning with those wonderful years working for the Arts Festival of Atlanta, one of the largest outdoor arts events in the US. Knowing my dreams and difficulties, you treated me like an artist. From your perusal of my book, you offered thoroughly considered comments and edits. Your intention centered on the best for the book and for me, and I'm so grateful you ignited fresh choices through your remarkable light.

To Jim Stratton, we realized an instant connection at a conference, becoming fast friends. A few years later, you not only evaluated the book, but you engaged with it, trying out the ideas and inspiration by journaling as you read. Once complete, we spent a weekend where you spoke from written notes in your copy of the manuscript. Thank you for the positive feedback, both conceptual and specific, and for leading me to strong revisions while boosting my self-assurance in speaking about the book.

My gratitude to the panel of beta readers for their distinctive viewpoints that reinforced my spirit and opened my mind to focus this work for a wide audience. Kim Peace Chamberlain, Karen A. Kroeger, Hana Njau-Okolo, and Ann J. Temkin were members of my Creative Writers' Workshop as well as coaching clients, and most still are. All are published. During our review discussion at the midpoint of my project, you were all thoughtful and innovative, while as a group, you were truly dynamic. To each of you, my deepest appreciation.

I'm thankful for two friends who were present at the beginning of my writing and coaching life, as well as being the final eyes on the book. Karen J. Vanderyt, you were the first student to arrive in my inaugural writing class which happened to be on Journaling. Soon thereafter, you became my first coaching client and have published four books with me over 20 years. During those years, our friendship solidified. And Martin J. Sargent, you were the first to attend a Writers' Forum I developed and cultivated where, along with you reading your superb essays, I read experimental pieces to mentor writers. We bonded through personal discussions on spirituality, writing, and life. Without forethought beyond each of your skills for proofreading, having the two of you close the circle on this project was profound since you both were instrumental at the inception of my writing this book. Kirby and Marty, I'm thankful for your generosity and our ongoing friendships.

To Kevin Gosselin, we met through a project for your uncle and my client Walt Prescott. Recognizing your talent, I encouraged you to design a cover for a novel and illustrate a children's book for other clients. When it was my book's turn, you enthusiastically collaborated as we improvised off my wildly scattered visions during fun, creative conversations. Then, one draft at a time, you produced extraordinary illustrations, and I felt the thrill of witnessing my first book's cover come to life. I am overjoyed and oh, so grateful.

To Kimberly Martin of Jera Publishing, you and I have worked on over twenty books through the years, developing an easy rapport. From trust in your work, the cover's elements, and my thoughts, you designed the book's interior, and then seamlessly moved it through production of print and e-book, then onto sales sites. I am grateful for having your expertise on my book project.

To Teryl Jackson, just like when you took my actor's head-shots years ago, you provided a relaxed yet energetic shoot for my author photo. In addition to mastery with the camera, your stellar communication and detail orientation produced a wealth of exceptional photos to choose from. I'm elated with the results. Again, my many thanks.

To other dear friends, many writers themselves, I'm grateful for your participation in nurturing conversations and offering retreats, giving wings for ideas to hatch and fly. Cindy Beckler, Dora Long Hayes, Lee Horsman and Lamar York, Louisa Merchant, and Kurt G. Schreiber, every one of you enjoyed discussing writing's process for journaling and memoir with me. And in your own special way, you continue to lift me in my writer's life, a gift I'm so grateful for.

My heartfelt appreciation to every person who joined me in the exploration of creativity, personal growth, and writing through journaling and other genres in workshops, classes, seminars, and coaching. I am thankful for every interaction as each enhanced the spectrum of our growing imagination and talents.

I am also grateful to those who planted seeds into my Never Mind. Every one gave me a challenge to strengthen my affirmative thinking and fortify my serenity while supplying plenty of emotions and prompts for journaling. Though sometimes difficult, these always brought abundant gifts and eventual thanks.

And to my angels, loved ones whose nourishing optimism now lives only in my thoughts, memories, and written words. Mom and Dad, thank you for encouraging my creativity and trusting my choices as I discovered and walked my path. Nanny and Papa, I'm grateful for your gift of providing a constant, affirming presence for my achievement with writing from a young age. And to my brother-from-another-mother, Emmett, thanks for sharing your unique perspective through episodes that tickled, confounded, and invigorated me, sometimes happening all at once, showing me ways to open up and live creatively in each moment. You all remain with me in every breath and keystroke.

Thanks to every one of you for bolstering my confidence and belief in myself. Your persistent, kindhearted support inspired and empowered me to write and publish this personal book. I treasure, respect, and love you all.

About the Author

Wayne South Smith is a writing coach, editor, public speaker, and published writer. Since 2003, he's followed his goal to build upon and share this experience. In his chosen work, he feels the potential of creative growth and expression in each moment, answering its call while inviting others to join him in a dynamic process of cultivating creativity in a writer's consciousness and practice, whether writing for an audience or themselves.

As a coach to writers from preteens to elders, Wayne focuses his skills and intuition on the writer and their writing. Writers have conquered blocks and fears while gaining a confident writing habit, successfully publishing books—novels, memoirs, inspirational, self-help, and children's picture books—alongside short stories, plays, and blogs, all on a broad range of topics. He's guided students toward successful college application and scholarship essays while teaching writing to enhance their education and career. For professionals, Wayne coached writers to books, portfolios, and speeches.

In workshops, classes, and seminars, he supports the synergy of the group along with the growth of the individual. These have been presented at universities, school systems, public libraries, writers' associations, arts centers, senior communities, and private gatherings.

Just as he encourages others, Wayne remains a motivated student. Life mirrors lessons and brings growth opportunities for which he is grateful. He finds coaching writers, alongside his own writing, as a powerful balance for his creative passion. Additionally, he credits his daily journaling, a cherished practice since 1987, as a fundamental catalyst, fueling growth both as a writer and human.

A graduate of the University of Georgia's School of Journalism, he earned a Bachelor of Arts in Broadcast / Film with minors in Drama and Speech. Wayne's features have been published in national and regional magazines, as well as local newspapers. He has also written scripts for film, stage, and puppet theater; authored web copy, marketing, and instructional materials; and penned fiction and creative nonfiction short stories.

After mentoring writers from inspiration to publication with over fifty books, *Writing Spirit: Journaling for Creativity and Personal Growth* is his first published book.

Wayne, a native Georgian, lives in Atlanta. For more information or to contact Wayne, visit waynesouthsmith.com.